The Small Hours of Belief

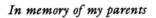
In memory of my parents

Enda McDonagh

The Small Hours of Belief

Meditation, Prayer and Preaching

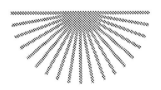

THE COLUMBA PRESS
DUBLIN 1989

THE COLUMBA PRESS
93 The Rise, Mount Merrion,
Blackrock, Co Dublin, Ireland

Designed by Bill Bolger
Origination by The Columba Press
Printed in Ireland by Genprint Ltd, Dublin.

ISBN 0 948183 68 3

The author and publishers are grateful to the following for
permission to use their copyright material: Macmillan, Basing-
stoke and London for *Suddenly* and *Absence* by R S Thomas; Angus &
Robertson for *Credo* by James McAuley; Faber & Faber for *In
Memory of W B Yeats* by W H Auden and for *a bespangled clown* by
e.e.cummings; Harper & Row Inc for *Autumn* by Rainer Maria
Rilke; Anvil Press Poetry for *Their Going, Their Dying* by Thomas
McCarthy; The Goldsmith Press for *God in Woman* by Patrick
Kavanagh and for *Buíochas/Gratitude* by Máirtín Ó Díreáin; Koz-
mic Press Centre for *The Evangelist John in the Wilderness* by Illya
Bukstein; The Blackstaff Press for *Hymn to a Broken Marriage* by
Paul Durcan; Eavan Boland for *Growing Up*; Francis Stuart for
The Love, The Loss, The Dream.

Our gratitude is due also to the editors of *The Furrow, Doctrine
and Life* and *The Mayo Year Book* where some chapters of this book
originally appeared as articles.

We have done our best to trace copyright on all material quoted in
this book. If we have failed to do so accurately we apologise and
invite copyright holders to contact us so that matters can be put to
right in future editions.

Contents

Introduction

Christian faith is finally the refinement of a life-time of struggle. But who is to say when that final refinement is achieved? Or, more properly, given? There may be markers, for high tide and low tide. These are usually unpredictable and unstable although the lows can seem more persistent and more frequent to one struggling believer. The ebb and flow recorded in this collection occurred mainly in the last few years. And they were usually provoked by particular events, ecclesial, political and personal, as they were frequently responses to requests to preach or pray or meditate.

As faith is in origin gift, so it is in practice response. The divine originator of the gift operates through human mediators, family and friends, neighbours and needy, church and cultural or political community. These human mediators of the divine gift often appear as simple seekers of human response in marriage homily or occasional prayer or publishable reflection. In the doing and the responding there emerges the believing. It may well be a broken believing. Indeed the believing may be in the breaking. Vulnerable to human need and request, the would-be believer can find faith unexpectedly surging in response. As if the demands and the demanders were also the bestowers of that presence and power which now and urgently seek expression. If one were never asked to preach or pray or meditate how would one believe? And how would one know whether and what one believes?

This book provides a record of provoked, and so bestowed, acts of belief. The 'small hours' carries obvious resonances and associations from the brief liturgical periods of the hours of the office, almost insistent renewals of prayer and presence, to the pre-dawn darkness and absence afflicting the sleepless, the depressed and the pathological self-doubters. Job and Jeremiah cursing the day they were born have their successors close to hand, and still more within cursing distance. Few christians can hope to escape these bleak small hours of darkness. And a proximate dawn cannot be guaranteed. Yet dawns do come. Not all of them brilliant and refreshing. The light can also be hard to bear.

The light and darkness at play in the fragments and more extended features collected here, reflect a life of belief, half-belief and unbelief. The mixture is by no means unique. Yet the belief persists and mainly prevails. The particular expressions of that belief reflect some of the practical shape of that life. Together with regular academic work and irregular, but demanding and fulfilling, pastoral counselling, directly preaching on the Word of God offers a constant challenge. Much of this occurs as a matter of course in parish or house-masses, at baptisms, weddings and funerals. These are too informal or fleeting or personal for publication. Other sermons, specifically requested for special occasions of a public kind, allow the preacher, through publication, the opportunity to share with a less intimate audience his struggles to respond in faith to more public joys and sorrows. A number of these sermons are included here.

The section 'Preaching' seeks to present practical examples in a wider theological setting, to underline the faith-struggles involved. The 'Risks of Preaching' reflects on the practice itself as at least one preacher experienced it. The concluding piece to this section, on 'Preaching and Conversion', is from an earlier date. It stresses the role of the preacher as participant in the community, listening to the world and summoned with that community to conversion.

Good preaching is the fruit of persistent prayer. Only one aspect of prayer is considered here. 'Prayer as Poetry' and 'Poetry as Prayer' are ancient themes, at least as ancient as the psalms. They have taken on increasing significance for me in recent years. This has been evident in teaching, preaching and working. A good deal of time is devoted to reading poetry, primarily for pleasure, enjoyment with enlightenment but as an end in itself. The reading, often aloud, has sometimes moved spontaneously and unconsciously into prayer. A more deliberate and self-conscious approach was encouraged some years ago when *The Furrow* initiated a series, 'Pray This Poem'.

While I got very few ready for publication, I kept up the exercise in private, sometimes written, sometimes not. Some further written ones are included here. They are practical instances to which *From Poetry to Prayer* provides some reflective introduction, written as it should be, after the practice was established.

The major concern of this book is 'Meditation'. It provides the framework for the book as a whole. For the functioning theologian, meditation is the usual mediator between intellectual and spiritual life, in so far as the two dimensions can be clearly distinguished. These pieces, labelled 'meditation' here, were born in very different circumstances, as their titles and attributions indicate.

Some ordering of them seemed useful. People (and their primacy) and places (of composition) suggest central concerns. People have always been central. For this reason, the very first part of this book is entitled 'Personal Engagements'. Places have emerged more recently as focal points for religious reflection. People at the fringe have been dominant in much recent christian theologies and meditations.

And death we have always with us. For so many it provides, in person or by proxy, the risk of diminishing belief, a very small hour indeed. The reflections here, originally presented to a medical-scientific congress, are intended to alert us to what should and can be the great hour of belief.

These scraps of life and fragments of vision are far from the twelve baskets of provisions which all of us in our spiritual malnutrition will continue to require. They may alleviate some immediate hunger for somebody. Above all they may send readers in search of more substantial food and a regular diet of proper meditation, prayer and preaching.

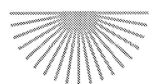

PART ONE

Meditation: *Personal Engagements*

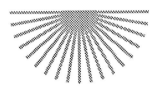

The Priest as Christian

If we didn't exactly believe that we had finally shed our former human condition on June 19, 1955, we certainly believed that an irrevocable change had taken place and that a whole new life was beginning. So it had and so it was. But somehow, thank God, the old human condition persisted and after twenty-five years it shows no sign of disappearing. We had been warned. Occasionally indeed we felt as if we had been threatened. 'The Church is a hard mother', we were assured, and discouragement was given more direct expression with the frequent reminder that lots of new jobs were opening up in Bord na Mona and that the front gate was always open. On the very day of ordination itself our senior mentor threatened, for the third successive year, to call the whole thing off because of some disruption of the preliminary rubrics.

But the Holy Spirit and the Archbishop of Dublin prevailed. The class of '55 walked down the aisle of the college chapel at about 10.30am and out through the great western doors into the wind and rain and fickle sunshine of a typical ordination Sunday at Maynooth. The scattering had already begun with those called back to their dioceses for ordination. Thrown together rather arbitrarily seven years before, we had, under pressure of wind and rain and the open gate, attained a taken-for-granted class spirit and formed a range of friendships that the immediate dispersal and fitful contact over the years would never entirely dissipate. Twenty-five years on (and, for some, 25 lbs on) the bonds are still palpable and the memories mainly cheerful. This, however, is not intended as an exercise in nostalgia but as some disjointed notes on how the 'irrevocable change' and 'new life' now appear to one silver jubilarian.

The trust and the trustee
Ordination and first Mass constituted a single dramatic production, somewhat complicated by the two 'first' Masses of those years, at Maynooth and then at home. In the liturgical ethos

of the time one tended to feel fully and properly a priest as one celebrated first Mass and particularly the home 'first'. The sense of what had been entrusted to one, of the trust received, was rendered somehow tangible in taking up the bread and wine at consecration and distributing the bread at communion. The summons not to betray that trust, to try to be worthy of what one handled, was a powerful feature of priestly spirituality then as it is now. In twenty-five years, trust and trusteeship have emerged more clearly as marking the ways of God with men and women, and the way of men and women with one another. Inevitably they bear a deeper significance, born of richer and sometimes sadder experience. However, they still revolve around the self-entrusting of God to humankind, realised to its full in the life and death of Jesus Christ and recalled and represented under the leadership of the priest at Mass.

It is hard to focus the great and gracious mystery of God entrusting God's self to humankind. The story called salvation recounts the continuing divine initiative as God places himself at the disposal of human beings, with all the risks and realities of betrayal and rejection. The experiment of Jesus Christ, of sending his own Son, exposed the length to which God as trusting Father was finally prepared to risk, the betrayal he was prepared to accept. Attentive to the New Testament, priests and christians generally could begin to appreciate the infinitely gentle, infinitely suffering pursuit by God of his plan for healing and transforming friendship with humankind. The gospel record of Jesus' life, continually poised between glory and destruction, from the praise of angels and slaughter of innocents to the final condemnation and death as a criminal, and acceptance on the cross by a fellow criminal, charts the course of human weakness and malice in face of divine trust and vulnerability. If anyone will come after him, he must expect the same reaction. The christian is not above his master. For all his special role, the priest is called primarily to be a christian, a disciple of Jesus Christ, sharing the glory and the destruction, or at least the joy of acceptance as well as the pain of rejection.

The joy can be overwhelming and humbling. The trust invested in one as a priest by so many people can be exhilarating and frightening. One is progressively overwhelmed by their painful honesty in diverse situations from confessional to casual travel-companionship on train or plane; their respect for the role of

priest; their self-entrustment to the person; their hopes of understanding, acceptance, enlightenment, consolation, forgiveness.
These slowly reveal themselves as basic human and christian needs
and activities while they clearly transcend human and christian
capacities and responses. Their true model and final significance
can only be found in the self-entrusting of God in Jesus, now expressed in christian sacrament and human person. Human actions
and experiences of trust realise and reveal, however weakly at
times, the fundamental trust by which God became involved in
human history. In his preaching and teaching, pastoral care and
sacramental celebation, the priest seeks to promote those experiences of human trust and link them with the foundational trust of
the Father, manifested in Jesus.

Continuing divine trust and human trust in face of misunderstanding, betrayal or rejection constitute the glory of human
history. Jesus' disciples, their community the Church and that
community's leaders, must all bear witness to and realise in their
lives, something of this glory. One useful test of our discipleship
as laity, religious, priests or bishops, would be: how far do we trust
one another? How far do we share the open, vulnerable trusting of
Jesus of Nazareth and of his heavenly Father? In our official
capacities we are tempted to be zealously controlling, if not un-
consiously power-seeking. With a sense of responsibility for the
salvaton of 'our' people or the formation of 'our' students we become over-protective, demanding trustworthiness of people
whom we do not trust. The unredeemed situation in which we all at
least partially live, is characterised more by distrust than by trust.
The Church and its representatives too often appear, in personal
response and official activity, to endorse that unredeemed and un-
redeeming distrust.(Perhaps that is why so few of us are crucified
today.) Too many interchanges between bishops, priests and people lack honesty and trust and their constant companion, vulnerability, the capacity and willingness to be hurt in one's trusting.

Without a share in that capacity and willingness, our
celebration of the trusting surrender of Jesus Christ in the Mass
will be greatly impoverished. Not to have trusted deeply and continuously and not to have suffered in one's trusting and still gone on
trusting, is to be deprived of a significant christian experience and
grace.

Love and Loneliness
Although love and the teaching and following of Jesus Christ

are so intimately and inseparably connected, we always had a certain hesitancy about speaking of love in a priest's life. Of course we spoke frequently, perhaps too frequently and too easily, of his love of God and sometimes, in a rather restricted sense, of his loving care of people. These are authentic aspects of the loving priest's life which require fuller explanation and continuing cultivation. But the loving priest! What's he like? What constitutes his love-life? After twenty-five years do we find ourselves more or less loving? Are we resigned, reserved and apathetic in our personal relations? Or soured and cynical? Or still adolescent and uncomfortably shy or foolishly flirtatious? How can we combine warmth and sensitivity with strength and constancy in relationships and responses?

The priest's problems about loving are undoubtedly bound up with his celibacy. Some of our contemporaries found these problems so intractable that they resigned the ministry in order to marry. And some of these, personally known to me, seem personaly enriched by marriage in the whole range of their loving relationships. But as marriage does not always work or make people more loving, neither is celibacy incompatible with making people loving and lovable. The sacrifice involved in celibacy, which is a sacrifice of the total richness of family love and life with wife and children, carries a loss and a pain that are never entirely transcended. That loss and pain are expressed in different ways at different stages of life. The pain of the more obvious sexual needs and desires may be moderated with time and yield to the more subtle and disturbing pain of lack of the fullness of companionship and friendship in a wife, lack of the excitement and hope for the future generated by children. Loneliness becomes more painful than sexual privation. It is well to recognise that there is no adequate human solution to either, although it is also well to recognise that both limitations are shared widely by other people, single, widowed, separated or still formally living in marriage.

In an important and felt sense, celibacy is a negation and a privation. The loss is something humanly valuable and it cannot be simply replaced or substituted for. The negation and privation enter into the witness or sign value of celibacy, raising at least a question-mark about the finality and completeness of human living and loving at its apparently most self-contained, husband and wife with children. With that question-mark, christian celibacy signals the transcendent kingdom, the only one in which final human fulfilment is available. The celibacy of discipleship is for the sake of the kingdom, as sign of it and in service of it. The sign and the service will be truly christian only if they are born of and express the heart of the kingdom, love. Celibacy is a way of loving, not simply of loving God but of loving the neighbour. These two loves are inseparable for christians. Loving the neighbour cannot be confined to some abstract good will or benevolence, or to some concrete but detached good deed or beneficence. It involves the whole person with his whole heart and his whole soul. It is a matter of feeling as well as of willing and doing. Christian love of neighbour is also genuinely human love.

The human and christian loving of celibates will vary enormously. Even the most fleeting contacts should experience something of the availability and freedom to love and to care which celibacy is intended to provide. The collaboration and companionship of colleagues in the ministry and fellow-workers in the parish can test anyone's loving capacity through the competitiveness, petty jealousies, mindless gossip and sheer incompatibilities, but the testing is necessary for the growth. Working in a parish, university or seminary rapidly exposes the limitations of one's loving and one's lovableness. It is hard to recognise and accept that people do not obviously love or like us and that there are people we cannot easily love or like, but it is an essential part of growing up and of learning really to love.

Over the years, working in Ireland and abroad has produced scores of enriching and lasting friendships. In the context of shared work and interests a companionship, trust and love developed which at least mitigated the loneliness and provided supports and challenges which both summon and enable one to go on. Naturally some of these relationships become more important than others. Close and permanent friendships emerged in which the sharing of work and ideas, while still important, was less significant than the sharing of selves. Whether with family members or old school friends or permanent colleagues or fortuitous acquaintances, the flowering of such friendships has proved critical to understanding the humanity and christianity of the priest. Without friendship it would be difficult to survive as a trusting and loving human being summoned to preach and realise the trusting and loving God of Jesus Christ. With close friendship there are difficulties also, hurt and misunderstanding, exploitation and neglect, which are only slowly and painfully overcome. The freedom of the priest for the people of God should not suffer through his particular friendships. His friends, like his family, have to recognise and respect that freedom. Yet without his friends and family he could not enjoy the inner freedom and achieve the liberation which makes him lovingly available to the people he serves.

Surprised by prayer

The priest, it was impressed upon us, must be a man of prayer. 'A holy priest makes a holy people and a priest who is not holy is not only useless but harmful.' The rising pitch of the voice of our spiritual director, Father Tom Cleary, still echoes in our ears. We have gone our different ways in following these directions over the years. It is difficult to be satisfied with the efforts made or results achieved. But what is more evident now than it was in the seminary is that prayer happens, at least occasionally and often surprisingly. It may be in the more easily anticipated setting of the Mass or the confessional or the sick call. One is no longer having to make the effort, keep the concentration or attend in faith because, suddenly and even startlingly, prayer occurs or, more accurately, the presence of God occurs. The experience may be short, subsequent memory vague, verification impossible but also unnecessary. The occurrence is naturally more surprising in less obvious contexts, from driving the car to reading a newspaper or novel to chatting to a friend. This is no great mysterious and mystical experience. The human roots of it no doubt lie in early education, seminary formation and some continuing effort at prayer and reflection. But it is so startling and refreshing as it occurs that it deserves more attention in our thinking and talking about prayer and in our attempts to improve the prayer-life of ourselves and others.

Three elements in the experience are worth emphasising. The occurrence itself is not anticipated, provoked or projected by the person. It happens to him. The initiative lies with God. Prayer is his gift. Secondly, while the prayer is of God and cannot be commanded or even anticipated, the way of life and effort at prayer do, in general, bear on its frequency and intensity. One cannot establish any exactly proportionate relationship between human effort and prayer even of this kind. Yet there seems to be a readiness required in the person if he is to be open to the event and grasp its significance. Thirdly, that relevance is related to sensitivity to

other human beings as well as to attention to prayer forms. There
is no question of opposing one to the other or pursuing one at the
expense of the other. Yet in priests and religious there may be a
danger that their prayer-block derives from the inhumanity of
their relationships rather than from their inattention to prayer.
The awareness of and sensitivity to human others, in their particular human mystery and in their unique participation in the ultimate mystery of God, create the psychological and theological
conditions in which one may be surprised by prayer.

Is there life after fifty?

Twenty-five is as artificial a dividing line as twenty-one or
thirty-two. Yet we need markers. Twenty-five years a priest may be a
useful marker. For many of us it will coincide with the approach of
a fiftieth birthday. All very sobering and solemn. What new ideas,
fresh energy, effective trusting and loving can one expect from
anybody after fifty? So we might have asked in 1955. It looks rather
different now. And it looks different partly because the intervening years have been fulfilling and enjoyable in ways we never anticipated, while the ways of pain and frustration were equally surprising. No doubt the joy and the pain will go on but they will, we
hope, continue to be the joy and pain of living more fully.

The Grace of Remembering

The first news of Gerry Meagher's death generated confusion. It reinforced one's own sense of fragility that a younger contemporary should die so quickly and so unexpectedly. The prevailing sense was one of loss and diminution. The loss was first of all personal. Gerry Meagher had among other significant qualities a loyalty to his friends, an understanding of differences and a nice appreciation of the ironies of life. These are not replaceable in the life of a person *d'un certain age*. The diminution was both personal and communal. We are all diminished by the death of a man of whom the key-word in belated tributes was courage. Without Gerry Meagher there will be less open and persistent questioning of conventional and established positions. The honesty and freedom which his courage promoted may easily be lost to us. They may yet be maintained and even enhanced if we remain vulnerable to the grace of remembering.

Death is the great simplifier. By cutting through the complexities and qualifications, the dependency, the rivalry and the resentments attendant on all human relations, it compels a new appreciation of the dead. This is no pious *nil nisi bonum* but attention, through simplification, to the central qualities and causes of deceased friend (or foe). It produces a new stage of friendship, in the ever-necessary conversion of friend to friend, while at the same time it proclaims the end of normal friendship. The relationship now depends on memory, that notoriously fitful and fickle, yet essential, capacity of the human being to incorporate the formative past into the developing present and future. The experience of friendship leaves its permanent mark. The memory of a friend can be consoling, encouraging and even inspiring as one appreciates anew his qualities and causes. But the nagging question persists: Is that all there is, memories, and increasingly vague memories? The 'merely memories' response does not do justice to the gift or grace of remembering or to its significance in the christian understanding of life and death.

Remembering Jesus Christ

Remembering is at the heart of the gospel message and events. The Jewish people from whom Jesus came, were formed by their remembering the mighty deeds of Yahweh. Abraham, Isaac and Moses, their judges, kings and prophets, continued to be formative figures in the life and liturgy of Israel. Jesus frequently invoked them and set about establishing his own identity and mission in relation to them. He had not come to destroy but to fulfil. Their memory, which embodied Yahweh's promise, achieved completion in the work and person of Jesus Christ. His memory in turn embodied the promise of final fulfilment when he would come again in glory. That memory and promise of Jesus Christ provide the key to understanding the memory and promise of our departed friends and family.

There were a great many people with good reason to remember Jesus in the aftermath of his death. Caiaphas and Annas and their Jewish friends were unlikely to have forgotten him overnight. Pilate who washed his hands of him, the Roman centurion who was so impressed and no doubt other members of the Roman court and soldiery retained, however briefly, their own memories of their gentle and gentlemanly victim. The crowds who were cheering on Palm Sunday and must have overlapped with those jeering at the weekend may have dismissed Jesus as a disturbing failure but could scarcely have entirely forgotten him by the following Sunday. But all their remembering, hostile or indifferent or impressed for the moment, was not the remembering of the disciples whom he had, according to John, finally described as friends. The remembering of his friends, after the shattering and simplifying experience of his death, included as well as a sense of loss, the pain of hope disappointed. As the disciples on the way to Emmaus put it: 'We had hoped that he was the one to redeem Israel' (Lk 24:21).

Yet it was that remembering which prepared the way for the recognition of his new presence. The risen, unlike the historical, Jesus was accessible only to his disciples, his friends. His new presence and their remembering met in that moment of recognition as retailed, for example, in the exclamation 'My Lord and my God', by the doubter Thomas. As loving memory and presence meet, conversion to the full reality of Jesus is completed. He stands before the throne of God as their mediator and intercessor. The mediation is available to those with loving and believing memory. Their celebration of the Eucharist in memory of him enables further encounters between remembering and presence once the post-Easter appearances have ceased. For the remembering was carried on in word and sacrament, in preaching and teaching, in baptism unto his death and eucharistic sharing of his new life. That first and critical remembering was recorded for future generations in the gospels and given shape for living in the other books of the New Testament. That record of remembering is vital to us, his current disciples, so that we may experience the conversion to his presence which the first disciples enjoyed in their special way. A special way because they had a direct remembering to call on, although the conversion of Paul already vindicates the power and the presence of Jesus beyond the immediate band of his remembering disciples.

We remember Jesus by entering into the remembering of his first disciples, and so he becomes present to us in his new presence to the Father. The Father is present to us as Father because we have joined the brotherhood of his Son, Jesus Christ. As disciples, friends and brothers of Jesus we are open to his mediating and interceding power with the Father. By putting on the mind of Jesus the Christ, by adopting his cause as our cause, in remembering him we become Christ-like. The loving power and presence of God as Son becomes available to us as adopted sons, remade in the image of Christ. Such memory far transcends 'merely memory' by the transforming power of God who raised Jesus from the dead and made him permanently and truly present to those who remember him as he really was and is. And this provides the clue to how we remember a friend in faith as he truly was and is.

Remembering as mediation

That he is and truly is in the presence of God is part of our faith in God and in our friend. The simplification of death helps to clear our minds to see more truly, just as it provides for him the way into his true self in the presence of the Father. Our remembering is the channel by which this presence to the Father touches us. It is the way our dead friend or parent reaches us by the power of the Father. It is how the Father reaches us through the channel of our friend. Our particular mediator-friend reaches us as we remember in faith and love his true self and share his cause. To benefit by his presence to God we have to recall in love his historical presence on earth. He becomes the channel of that particular grace which characterised his own person and his own struggle for those who appreciate the person and share the struggle, whether before his death or by subsequent conversion.

The Church, in venerating the saints, has always paid great attention to the specific shape of their christian lives. St Francis, St Ignatius and St Teresa of Avila were not saintly in some general sense but, in their personalities and lives, they provided new and original embodiments of discipleship. People who are drawn to these saints, inspired by their particular character and achievements, have devotion to them and remember them prayerfully. It is this admiring, sympathetic and prayerful remembering which leads people to look to their saints as particular intercessors before God. It is sympathy with the persons and causes of these saints which enables the living to be open to the particular mediation of God which takes place through these saints. Remembering is the living link with the 'communion of saints'. It maintains contact with those who have gone before and sensitises the living to the Franciscan or Ignatian or Teresian graces. To take one example, as a counter-witness of poverty in an affluent, self-indulgent society, the radical way of St Francis has continuing validity and attracts ever new followers and imitators. They are the people for whom his particular presence to God is fruitful. In their remembering Francis and commitment to his cause, they are open to the divine grace which is mediated through him. He is a kind of sacrament. In the old sense he is a channel of particular sacramental, Franciscan grace; in contemporary theology he is a locus of the divine/human encounter with its specific Franciscan shape.

The death of a friend is a loss and a painful loss. His memory enshrines his true value, his spirit and his cause. In the christian context that memory enables us to reach him still, not just as he was but as he is in the presence of God. In that presence the courage and all the other rich qualities that were Gerry Meagher's become grace, a mediation of the power of God, to those who knew and remember him lovingly. The awkward questioner of smooth arrangements, or the persistent promoter of justice for colleagues and students is no longer audible. That silence will always be sad. Yet the grace of remembering enables us to work for similar goals, inspired by his past example and sustained by his new and mediating presence before the face of God.

Women, Friends and God

'I would, if I could, write new words for women.' P.J. Kavanagh's poetic aspiration, pursued in prose in the beautiful auto-biographical account of his first marriage, A Perfect Stranger, might well be adopted by theologians, church leaders and christians generally. This is not a meditation on sexist language and the christian need to replace it, urgent as that task is. Neither is it a meditation on the broader concerns of feminist theology or the still broader feminist movements, within and without the Church. Their significance and urgency must here be taken for granted. And their implications will undoubtedly affect the shape and flow of these reflections and may well return in criticism of their language and spirit.

Meditations, and certainly this one, should aim to be more personal than scholarly, more fruit of experience and commitment than of study and critical analysis. What is in mind here is the expression of what is in life and has been in life over a long time.

For all the pastoral, academic and social concerns and engagements, friendship has proved a powerful influence in sustaining, healing, developing and transforming every dimension of my life. Such friendships go back to beginnings, to family and neighbours and schoolmates of earliest memory. Many of these, thank God, still play a significant role. Many others have come later. Many have gone to death and separation by geography or history, by erosion or conflict. But it is now, as it was in the beginning, impossible to give an account of self, to describe or even identify self apart from friends and friendships. For somebody who accepts love of neighbour as mediating and reflecting love of God, friendship is crucial to faith and faith-reflection or theology.

One of the lessons of a life-time of friendships is the need to distinguish friends and allies for particular causes. This might be better expressed in terms of friends with differences. One cannot expect one's friends to agree with all one's positions in religion or theology, politics, the arts or all the thousand interests and engagements humans are heir to. Friendship with differences is not always easy to maintain. And the question of limits undoubtedly arises. Could one remain on friendship terms with a rampant racist? Mostly the limits are too narrowly defined. Personal likes and dislikes combine too easily with personal ambitions in alliances of people of similar attitudes and activities on religious, social and political issues. The network of different and so mutually-enriching friends is reduced to the tribal defensive circle of loyalists. There are too many obvious examples of this in and between churches, social groups, academic institutions, political parties and movements to require further rehearsal here. Apart from the human deprivation, suspicion and hostility which such tribalism involves, it provides clear counter-witness to God's generous offer in Jesus of friendship for and with all. The christian thrust is essentially anti-tribal.

This digression from the central concerns of this particular meditation helps underline the difficulties, the potential and the necessity of friendships between the deeply different. Friendships between men and women belong in this category. Friendships between women and celibate men seem significant instances of the difficulties of friendship between the deeply different. The difficulties are, to some extent, those of conceptualisation and categorisation. The most ordinary, pervasive and so powerful dimensions of human life are not readily conceptualised and categorised. Such difficulty in thought and expression does not necessarily include difficulty in doing or, indeed, in knowing intuitively or practically what to do and how to do it. Loving is notoriously incapable of adequate conceptualisation and expression. Friendship as a form (the form?) of loving is subject to the same difficulties. Both love and friendship find more adequate expression in artistic forms than in intellectual analysis. Love-story and love-poem provide the best verbal access to love-meaning.

Meditation hovers somewhere between the narrative and the analytic. In its higher forms it may come close to the poetic. Shakespeare's soliloquies were meditative poetry. Many other great poems share this meditative quality. The excitement of intense love-lyrics may shatter the calm expected of meditation but their spirit may nurture the reflections of the more restrained and less gifted lyrically.

The influence of personal history, the story of one person's friendships, enters closely into this meditation. Less directly, a life-time's interest in threatre, words and poetry will have influenced the learning process as it wrestles with the meaning of love and friendship, and in particular with the love and friendship which I, as a celibate male, have enjoyed with women friends.

The revealing and concealing which such reflection involves is not a matter of simple, deliberate choice. Apart from the conscious demands of discretion in protection of others and of the self, a great many unconscious and uncontrollable influences are bound to be at work. The writer himself will not be able to judge fully how far he is revealing or concealing. The search for honesty is essential but always incomplete. And the need to provide some broader insights rather than personal reminiscences, as the goal of meditation, could render the whole exercise banal. Yet as a form of self-understanding, as a tribute to friends and above all as a possible help to a wider readership, these risks of self-deception, indiscretion and banality seem worth taking.

The multi-layered person which composes any of us at a particular stage in life, carries the deposits of infancy and childhood, adolescence and adulthood. So the conventional psychological wisdom has it. And these are not necessarily submerged layers. The squalling and delighting infant, the tiresome and bold child, may suddenly combine with the eager and vulnerable adolescent in the responses and relationships of the would-be integrated and confident adult. Whatever friends are for, they may find, disconcertingly, that they have to cope with childish outburst or adolescent lapse. This may more easily, or at least more obviously, occur within marriage, given the day-long and life-long companionship. It may also occur in other, less intimate, friendships of the same sex or of different sexes. In meditating on relationships with women-friends and women-acquaintances, my inability to overcome, or better to integrate into dynamic adulthood, earlier processes and experiences, with their failures and hurts, their achievements and joys, creates continuing pain and confusion.

Friends as people are human and first of all a cause of rejoicing, a reason for giving thanks. That Yeats had such friends as the Municipal Gallery displayed may not be our first reason for remembering him. It was no doubt a genuine source of joy and satisfaction to himself. And at the risk of sounding patriarchal and patronising, a man must insist that women-friends are above all people and people-friends. The gift of people and of people friends is our most immediate source of faith-hope-love in human and christian terms. For that and for them we must continue to give thanks. Even in their demands on us, and their existence is demand as well as gift, they are potentially enriching as they draw us once again out of our narrow self-enclosing world to respond to their presence and identity, their richness and their need. Where presence and demand become dominantly a threat, and at times it does, the sinful, destructive side of one or both is intruding. Such sinfulness or destructiveness is an ineradicable part of all of us. It obstructs our final adult integration as friends and lovers, spouses and parents. For all its obstruction it need not dominate. Friendship, love and marriage can prevail as dominantly integrated and creative relationships.

The source of attraction and love, as of distraction and fear, between people is difference. The sexual difference is here pre-eminent. Attraction and love between the sexually different receive most of the good lines in gossip as in life, in fiction, poetry and drama as in fact. And this even where, as so often in story, the attraction and love issue in destruction and hatred. Distraction and fear are no less part of the human sexual interaction. For priests and religious they may well be the dominant features. Seminary isolation and training in the past often reinforced for priests the fear and sense of distraction. One of the oddities of the young priest's life was his sudden thrust into the role of father of all, without passing through the demands of parenting for any. Of course it provided a certain prestige and protection but it did not necessarily make for authentic relations with women old enough to be his mother and particularly with those young enough to be his wife. From cherished family-son to vulnerable parish-father did not always make for creative adult integration.

What my generation of priests missed for the most part was that crucial move from adolescent curiosity and experimentation, with inevitable failure and growth, to settled collaboration, partnership and friendship. Immediate family and neighbours, sisters, cousins and other contemporaries provided a feminine warmth and ease which even seminary isolation could not entirely root out. Natural attractions and harmless flirtations assisted the process of growth and maintained a certain balance between desire and fear, respect and intimacy.

Most of us have much reason to be grateful to a range of

women and girls who respected our sense of our calling and at the same time treated us as male human beings, even attractive human beings. And many of us would have serious doubts about how well and properly we responded. Further excavations would no doubt reveal hurts and failures about which we may still feel a certain shame.

Adolescent desire and fear did not disappear with ordination. Given our years of isolation they may well have gained in force in the setting of parish or school or university. The push to fatherhood, spiritual as it may have been, could not replace the slow, painful search for integrated, stable and loving relationships with women, for whom like Jesus, we hoped to be servants and friends.

The details and detours of earlier autobiography would constitute a distraction from the main concern of this meditation and a possible embarrassment to writer and readers. The child, adolescent, adult partner and spiritual parent still contend in life and relationship in ways that are illuminating as well as occasionally, at least, humiliating. The object of this reflection is primarily 'illumination'; this means some attention to the gifts and challenges of women who have become women-friends in a context in which friendship is finally founded in God.

The gifts and challenges of women-friends must not be separated from the gifts and challenges of men-friends. Humanity is a larger and more profound category than womanhood or manhood. Differences between human beings are often larger and more profound than the gender difference. Race and class, culture and history and all the dimensions of individuality provide an astonishingly enriching and challenging set of differences. These very differences enter into the unique persons of women and women friends, undermining any simple gender categorisation.

Gender remains a significant difference. A Maynooth with women, as well as men, among students and staff is profoundly changed from the single-sex institution of its first hundred and seventy years. Women-friends are different, at least for me, as I try to keep them clearly in mind and heart, as individual persons, human beings and friends.

The ideal description of such friends, younger, older and contemporary, might be that of loving or, to use the safer word, affectionate partners. The degrees of love-affection and of partnership-collaboration vary from person to person and from time to time, even for the same persons. Yet the two elements are essential and manifest themselves in a variety of ways. Shared interests are often the basis of origin and usually the source of continuity. But simple personal attraction, two people getting on well together, easily relating and freely recounting something of themselves, is as common a cause of friendship between priests and women as it is between other people. Such relating normally seeks some partnership expression. Celibacy, which may play a role in the attraction on either side, naturally restricts but does not exclude such partnership.

It is hard to describe, still harder to define, such a partnership. It can and does take a thousand forms. Some of my closest relationships have been with both wives and husbands, sharing in some of their hopes and frustrations as parents. For all that the friendship remains independent of the children and has its own particular shape in relation to both husband and wife. The love and the partnership are there but not easily distinguished, seldom explicit and never intrusive, I hope.

One particular advantage of this is to enable one to appreciate something of what fathering and mothering, or parenting, means. The demands and the satisfactions, the pains and the joys in which parent friends include one, illuminate and strengthen some aspects of one's own wider pastoral role. More deeply, they may open one a little more to God's loving and caring, the God who is father and mother to us all. Without the partnership of women-friends, priests and preachers are liable to miss much of the startlingly feminine in a humanity created in God's image and so miss much of God.

Partnership extends much beyond the happy accident of sharing in some of the family enterprise. Pastoral partnership between men and women is a developing aspect of the contemporary church. It will usually generate some affection and move into friendship. The same pattern is noticeable in academic, theological activities and in a host of political, social and cultural enterprises. Affectionate partnership may not always emerge. Colleagues don't have to be friends, at least not close friends. Yet in the christian way of things, respect between colleagues involves a care that usually needs sustaining by some affection if it is not to be destroyed by resentments and jealousies – a result too common in so many institutions of commerce, learning and even religion. In academic and religious institutions, for all the tensions and ambiguities I have observed, the advent of women-colleagues has tended to be humanising in a relational way as well as developing in a professional way.

The professional challenge and development of women-colleagues may be a new source of threat in Church or academy. The childhood dependence and resentment, the adolescent desire and fear are still so much part of male immaturity, that there may be a rush to defend the past bastions. My meditation leads in a related but slightly different direction, as I reflect on the influence of my women-friends.

The childishness which surfaces in adults, in this instance in adult men, can be demanding, irrational, insatiable. It can also be a necessary and welcome surrender of arms, a useful acceptance of one's weakness and fearfulness in a frightening world. Such lapses can be a challenge and sometimes a burden to one's family and friends. They can also draw from one's women-friends in particular a care and support that is mother-like, supportive and finally healing. That adult-men sometimes need mothering, when their mothers are no longer available, should be no more surprising than that adult women sometimes need fathering when their fathers are not available. Women-friends and priest-friends can and sometimes do fulfil those temporary roles.

The persistence of the adolescent dimension is no less real and sometimes no less threatening. The sexual curiosity, desire or fear do not quickly or ever entirely disappear. The re-assurance of steady friendship does help. Stabilised friends do not readily become sex-objects for the restless male in one. Of course risks remain within and without friendship. The erratic, erotic movements of one's maleness are not so easily and consistently integrated into responses to women-friends and acquaintances.

Beyond stable friendships which seek to reflect the best of one's early experiences, as well as the spiritual ideals of one's vocation, the insights of literature and art can be both revealing and healing. So many novels in my life seem to have operated as informers and integrators in the slow growth into truly living celibacy. At a later stage the tenderness, fragility and vulnerability of some of the great paintings of women have promoted a sense of joy and repose in them in their bodily forms which I could not have anticipated as an adolescent. Despite the cheap exploitation of so much advertising, the degrading thrust of the girlie-magazines and the horrors of the video-nasties, there is a sensibility to women in their sexuality evident in literature, painting, sculpture and film in which men should rejoice and by which they may be healed and integrated. For celibates this may at once liberate them for richer friendship and enable them to be more easily helped by their women-friends.

'I would, if I could, write new words for women.' It still seems dangerously romantic and yet totally inadequate for friends who as mother, sister-in-law, cousins, neighbours, colleagues, students and intimate partners have helped make sense of humanity and christianity in that angular and awkward male form, the celibate priest. Their God in all divine and feminine attributes be thanked.

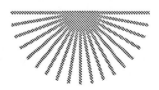

PART TWO

Prayer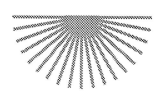

From Poetry to Prayer

Slow learning is a healthy exercise. Too often there isn't the time or the patience for that attention to narrative, ideas, people, which pains and pleasures by turn as it humiliates in weakness and transforms in grace. Reading poetry cannot be rushed. Neither can prayer. Of course, one is tempted to gabble both in mouth and in mind. But then gabble they remain. They lose all claim to authenticity. 'Heaping up empty phrases as the gentiles do' (Mt 6:7) is no more valuable in poetry than it is in prayer. The good poem stops one in one's tracks. It demands repetition. Only slowly and gradually does it take the reader over. He may skip and skimp with a novel or other narrative. To do so with poetry is to miss the point and the poem. With prayer, the skipping and skimping may appear less obvious. Not every word is so clearly the fruit of deliberate choice. Sound and rhythm are not such critical features. Indeed the best prayer may be soundless, beyond words and poetry. Yet the stopping short by the poem, its claim on one's exclusive and persisting attention to its detailed and complete world, offers a good parallel to the cry halt of prayer.

The parallels go further. The complete, self-enclosed world of the poem, transient as it may be, provides a shock and depth of awareness for the reader which real prayer, when it happens, resembles. And it happens, real prayer. It is not something which is primarily contrived or achieved, unless the waiting, the attentive, increasingly concentrated waiting, counts as contrivance or achievement. In a recent interview, retiring American Poet Laureate, Richard Wilbur, announced that he was returning to his quiet life in the country in the hope that poems would happen to him again. He was, of course, speaking of writing poetry.

Prayer can be like that too, a happening that takes shape or, rather, shapes the mind to the mystery. Spirit becomes word, takes flesh even as one reads and then stops reading.

And yet there is much labour as for every fine thing. The practice of prayer is certainly no easier than the practice of reading poetry. But the practice of reading poetry, in silence except for the sounding mind, or preferably aloud, can be an important part of the preparatory refining labour for prayer. In-labour for poem or prayer, or, more accurately for the non-poets among us, in-labour from poem to prayer, carries all the frustration and a little of the exhilaration to which the poetic and the prayerful are heirs.

Lest this all seem too fanciful, in the distorted poetic or de votional sense, I include a number of examples of poems leading to prayer. Lest the poverty of the examples damage irreparably the central thesis relating poetry and prayer, it is necessary to develop some further and deeper connections. 'Parallels' seems too weak a term for what seems intrinsic to the practice of reading poetry, and the practice of prayer.

There is a danger here that reading poetry and writing poetry will be confused as the same practice of poetry, and so obscure the relation of both to the practice of prayer, which itself includes reading or chanting of prayer as in liturgical prayer. For this writer and his readers, the reading of poetry as an exercise for its own sake, is the first concern. Its capacity to prepare people to pray depends on poem and reader. Personal experience suggests that readers may be opened by the poem to the world beneath or beyond its world within, that the beauty and truth pinned to paper by poet may mediate encounter with ultimate beauty and truth.

This 'sacramentality' of the poem, if one may use the term, has to be handled very carefully. The first respect is to be paid to the poem in itself. Its very existence and message, above all its shape and form, must be accepted as they are. A poem is not a means to prayer, any more than another human being is a means to loving God. Human beings must be loved for themselves, for their own sakes, not for Christ's sake or for God's sake. Only thus are they loved as God loves them; only thus is God loved.

The human creations called poems have their own fierce integrity. They may not be manipulated in some higher religious cause. Their connection with prayer, if it occurs for a particular reader, must issue from within the poem as it takes over and the reader surrenders to its power and beauty and truth. For a christian believer in creation, incarnation and liberation, the poem's potential to awaken the reader to the world and to the pain and final glory of the world makes good sense. When an authentic awakening occurs which does justice to the poem, it leaves the reader on the threshold of prayer. The further move into prayer is of grace building on grace. When the grace and gift of the poem encounters the graceful mind and heart of the reader, the rising of mind and heart to the mystery of mysteries may readily occur. Prayer, like Richard Wilbur's poem, may happen.

As I was writing this , I was simultaneously struggling with Seamus Heaney's *The Government of the Tongue*. Struggling seems an ungrateful and ungracious word in face of such a graciously written and enlightening book. Heaney had provoked some of these reflections earlier by sharply emphasising, in an interview, the distinction between poetry and prayer, in which, as I recall, he appeared to confine prayer to prayer of petition only, to asking for some good from some God. He does not address the problem directly in this book, but I take enormous comfort from his tracing various dualities, such as 'sound and sense'(Auden),'song and suffering' (Chekov et al), 'celebration and protest'(Herbert and so many other Eastern Europeans). All these would apply, I believe, very effectively to much of the Jewish and Christian prayer tradition. His remarkable treatment of Elizabeth Bishop's remarkable poem 'At the Fishhouses'(pp 102-107), with its 'daylight truth' and 'dream truth', displayed that shift from observation of the ordinary daily mysteries to the awareness of some extraordinary deeper mystery within. The seal 'interested in music' is one symbol of this. And then the powerful 'transmutation of fire' called water, 'tasting bitter, briny and burning your tongue like knowledge drawn from the hard cold mouth of the world', takes one into a new world-vision.

Poems have their own sudden change of vision and of world. The concentration and celebration which one reads oneself into, may shift unexpectedly to new light or dismay. The habits of the heart may be jolted out of a deadening routine to fresh and exciting possibilities. There is a conversion note here, conversion to a new vision certainly, even a new commitment. Not that poems have to emulate Amos, Isiah and Jeremiah, poets, social critics and mediators of a new vision of a new Israel and new creation, as they were. The examples of Mandelstam and Herbert demonstrate so effectively in Heaney's book, that the poem is the protest and prophecy in its very nature. The connections are there. Conversions are possible. A new humanity is signalled. The tyranny of social realism cannot, any more than that of individual consumerism, finally extinguish the human spirit, which is in itself holy, as wholly other than mechanical determinations of economics or politics. The human mystery persists. The mystery of the world still glimmers. The poets lead us to these kindly lights in an often unkindly and encircling darkness. In John's prologue, too, the Word was made flesh. Divine poetry took shape as the Spirit (Creation) overshadowed Mary. The light came into darkness which could not finally master it. Poetry as prelude to prayer and transformation has elements of the divine strategy about it. Grace and the Spirit enable and require human creativity as the continuous expression of the divine.

The prelude is not the play. If poetry must be respected for itself, so must prayer. And there are as many ways of prayer as of poetry, with undoubtedly some overlapping of classification in incantational, narrative and lyrical forms. Reading poetry may help prepare for all kinds of prayer, recited or created, oral or silent, lighted and imaged or dark and elusive.

Christian preparation for prayer, in life, habits of the heart and exercises of the mind, has always been regarded as crucial. And yet for Christians, prayer is primarily given rather than achieved, divine grace rather than human achievement. The preparation is that of the wise virgins awaiting the bridegroom. It is the attentive waiting on God which, under the urgings of the real if ungrasped divine presence, summons all the human resources of life and love, thought and word, to listen to, become possessed by and so express, that presence.

The Christian tradition has never been in doubt that we are enabled to achieve that simplest and most profound of prayers, calling God 'Abba, Father', by the Holy Spirit who has been poured forth in our hearts. It is God's Spirit who gives witness as we pray (Rom 8).

C. S. Lewis captured this paradox of our prayer as God's speaking through us in his effective poetic description:

Prayer

Master, they say that when I seem
To be in speech with you,
Since you make no replies, it's all a dream
– Or one talker aping two.
They are half-right, but not as they
Imagine; rather, I

Seek in myself the things I want to say
And lo! the wells are dry.
Then seeing one empty, you forsake
The listener's role, and through
My dead lips breathe, and into utterance wake
The thoughts I never knew.
And thus you neither need reply
Nor care; thus, while we seem
Two talking, thou art one forever, and I
No dreamer, but thy dream.

Not a great poem, but a valuable insight into the christian tradition of prayer at its best and at its most divinely given and
humanly creative. It has obvious connections with some traditional theories of poetic inspiration and composition. In his
discussion of Sylvia Plath's late Ariel poems, in The Government
of the Tongue, Seamus Heaney speaks of Sylvia Plath in her last
months as growing 'to a point where she permitted herself identi-
fication with the oracle and gave herself over as a vehicle for possession'(p 149). 'The great appeal of Ariel and its lyrics is the
feeling of irresistable given-ness'(p 151). 'We feel the poem as a
gift arising or descending beyond the poet's control, where direct
contact is established with the image-cellar, the dream-bank, the
word-hoard, the truth-cave – whatever place a poem like Yeats'
"Long-Legged Fly" emerges from'(p 163). The powerful poems
'Words' and 'Edge', quoted and analysed by Heaney here, would
easily lead one into the brooding that is prayer until the christian
reader at least might feel drawn to give oneself 'as a vehicle for
possession', not to some cave-dwelling power, but to the Spirit
who broods over the darkness and finally releases the light.

Uncritical, easy comparisons between poetic inspiration
and inspiration (in-breathing of the Spirit) in prayer can only
damage the integrity of both. Yet the rhythms of creativity, surrender and transformation do relate and resemble. The relations
and resemblances do not make the poet a person of prayer. They do
frequently reveal him as struggling with those dimensions of humanity and the world which the person of prayer must also address,
if he is to have access to the divine source and destiny of humanity
and the world.

Persons of prayer are not, as such, poets. Yet the achievements of the poets can lead them to the threshold of prayer,

sensitising them to those very dimensions of life which tremble on the verge of the divine. From poetry to prayer is one possible route for the prayerful Christian, as the following reflections may show. It can be quite an enriching one.

The Absence

It is this great absence
that is like a presence, that compels
me to address it without hope
of a reply. It is a room I enter
from which someone has just
gone, the vestibule for the arrival
of one who has not yet come.
I modernise the anachronism
of my language, but he is no more here
than before. Genes and molecules
have no more power to call
him up than the incense of the Hebrews
at their altars. My equations fail
as my words do. What resource have I
other than the emptiness without him of my whole
being, a vacuum he may not abhor?

R.S. Thomas

For the would-be prayer, R.S. Thomas can appear too easy a source. The preoccupation with religious themes, explicit or implicit, of the Welsh clergyman-poet can prove misleading as well as disconcerting. The bleakness of view, often just short of despair, provides no easy religious consolation. Yet his command of form, combined with religious depths of feeling, make his poems exhilarating as poetry and as experience at least of the darkness of faith. 'Absence' reflects that darkness in words resonant of the empty secularism to which we are all exposed.

Prayer

My God, as I still dare to say, I find this poem so attractive and yet so painfully elusive. I have some sense of the absence. Yet I am still overwhelmed by the petty presences: petty lusts and vanities, grandiose and pathetic schemes for reform. Even sober, useful activities in life and liturgy seem such distraction from the dark incomprehensible mystery that I need to experience as overpowering absence. I need to let the darkness be, to let the vacuum reveal the vacuity of all that I am and do. Only thus shall I be ready for the presence. And if the presence should not come, if you should not abhor the vacuum, will I be able for the real absence? How much darkness can I bear? Is this why you leave me with the protection of my petty presences? Let their pettiness at least remind me of the grandeur of the Absent. Or do I dare to ask for more?

Credo

That each thing is a word
Requiring us to speak it:
From the ant to the quasar,
From clouds to ocean floor –
The meaning not ours, but found
In the mind deeply submissive
To the grammar of existence,
The syntax of the real;
So that alien is changed
To human, thing into thinking:
For the world's bare tokens
We pay gold coin,
Stamped with the king's image;
And poems are prophecy
Of a new heaven and earth,
A rumour of resurrection.

James McAuley

The discovery of Australian poetry on a large scale has been an enriching experience. A visit there gave me a sense of a vibrant literary culture, with a growing number of fine novelists and poets. A very handsome volume, *Anthology of Australian Religious Poetry*, selected by Les A. Murray, has proved a great source of pleasure and prayer. James McAuley is strongly represented in this volume. Credo follows through the logic of literature and poetry: 'Each thing is a word/requiring us to speak it'. At another level this reflects the logic of creation 'in the mind deeply submissive to the grammar of existence'. Creation by human and divine word expose one to the logic of prophecy and 'a rumour of resurrection'.

Prayer

That we should speak thy world, O God, ant and quasar, clouds and ocean floor, is too much for minds struck dumb in childish wonder and yet ready to ignore in adult arrogance. Let us be true discoverers of meaning and truth, beauty and joy. Let minds submissive 'to the syntax of the real' recognise how 'the alien is changed to human' in the mysteries of creation and incarnation. And let the prophecy of this poem speak to us Emmaus-fashion, so that our hearts may burn with joy and hope at the first 'rumour of resurrection'.

In Memory of W. B. Yeats

You were silly like us: your gift survived it all;
The parish of rich women, physical decay,
Yourself; mad Ireland hurt you into poetry.

New Ireland has her madness and her weather still,
For poetry makes nothing happen: it survives
In the valley of its saying where executives
Would never want to tamper: it flows south
From ranches of isolation and the busy griefs,
Raw towns that we believe and die in; it survives,
A way of happening, a mouth.

W.H. Auden

W.H. Auden wrote his memorial tribute to Yeats in the month after the Irish poet's death in January 1939. The complete poem has a diversity and richness in form and content which this middle section alone could not convey. The section, in its attention to person and to poetry, to the silliness, the hurt and the futility, challenge the reader out of concentration on the icon, Yeats the mask, into awareness of 'that mysterious, always brimming lake' where all shall be renewed.

Prayer
Thanks be to God for the silliness, and for the reach of loving foolishness, by which your poet, at the end 'a tattered coat upon a stick', could find in 'the foul rag and bone shop of the heart' the beauty, the love, the pity.

Out of Irish chaos, Lord, your creative power drew art and artist, prophet and poet. Within continuing chaos, your gift of poets, with a creativity that tragically 'makes nothing happen', atones for executives who shirk the valley of imagination and feeling, of ecstasy and desolation, the valley of your incarnate humanity.

For us who 'hurt him into poetry', the regrets are ambivalent. The madness still with us we would repent. The grace of poetry that stretches from Ben Bulben to Byzantium we rejoice in and give thanks for. Minor players in this 'casual comedy', we seek refuge with you, Lord. From the 'ranches of desolation and the busy grief' let this poetry and your promise rescue us.

Autumn

Die Blätter fallen, fallen wie von weit
als welkten in den Himmeln ferne Gärten;
sie fallen mit verneinender Gebärde.

Und in den Nächten fällt die schwere Erde
aus allen Sternen in die Einsamkeit.

Wir alle fallen. Diese Hand da fällt.
Und sieh dir andre an: es ist in allen.

Und doch is Einer, welcher dieses Fallen
unendlich sanft in seinen Händen hält

&

The leaves are falling, falling as if from far up,
as if orchards were dying high in space.
Each leaf falls as if it were motioning 'no'.

And tonight the heavy earth is falling
away from all the other stars in the loneliness.

We're all falling. This hand here is falling.
And look at the other one....It's in them all.

And yet there is Someone, whose hands
infinitely calm, hold up all this falling.

Rainer Maria Rilke

Translation as betrayal is an objection not readily disposed of, at least in poetry. Robert Ply's translation here seems accurate, elegant and in the spirit of the poem. ('Calm' for 'sanft' in the last line seems a little off.) Yet for somebody with an ear for the original language, translations are seldom fully satisfactory. As prelude to prayer the original tones are more seductive. Yet the move to prayer involves its own translation and betrayal.

Rilke has been depicted (even self-depicted) as religiously unorthodox and hostile to the churches which 'encircle God as though he were a fugitive, and then bewail him/as if he were a captured wounded creature'. Yet his religious sensibility was very real, as this poem testifies.

Prayer
For us, O God, autumn is a state of being as well as a season, a mood of the human mind and soul as well as of trees and leaves. It is a melancholy mood, Lord, observing the falling leaves, earth and stars drop uncontrollably into the empty dead spaces of a graveyard world. Our letting go, falling away from the apparently necessary supports of place and pleasure, into the 'infinitely gentle hands' of you, O living and loving God, is no longer a fearful but a graceful destiny.

Their Going, Their Dying

There's a special sorrow that we reserve
For parents, so deep that the world of love,
The world of small happenings – of babies
Born and young wives undressing for a second
Time – cannot gain access.

Philosophy
Itself can hardly probe so deep. Only
The rain clouds bursting on mountains beyond
My writing window, leaves blown against glass
By the spirit of a storm, or a dog
Howling against the first frost of the year
Can reach the subjective hollow in the head.

Thus, the old impress our lives with their deaths,
Having borne us in pain to start the argument
And opened their love-filled hearts just too late
To leave us, abruptly, wondering where they went.

Thomas McCarthy

The rich range of contemporary Irish poetry offers many opportunities for joy and sorrow. Thomas McCarthy, one of the younger generation, provides, in his early book *The Sorrow Garden*, unusual awareness of death from one then so young.

Prayer
O God, who are ultimately Father and Mother to us, you know that without our earthly parents' presence and prayer, we could have made no sense of you or of ourselves. Their abrupt leaving left us 'hollow in the head' and heart. A limb or two had been cut off. We were forced to grow new ones, to grow up into the unsheltered storm and rain. And for the single and celibate, home was no longer there with them but had to be started anew here with you.

The 'special sorrow we reserve for parents' was a sorrow for ourselves too and for you, our God. Both had to be rediscovered and redefined as we wondered where our parents had gone and how we could keep in communication. In your mercy, God, let the lines of communication remain open – with them, with you, with our own real selves.

God in Woman

Now I must search till I have found my God –
Not in an orphanage. He hides
In no humanitarian disguise,
A derelict upon a barren bog;
But in some fantastically ordinary incog:
Behind a well-bred convent girl's eyes,
Or wrapped in middle class felicities
Among the women in a coffee shop.
Surely my God is feminine, for Heaven
Is the generous impulse, is contented
With feeding praise to the good. And all
Of these that I have known have come from women.
While men the poet's tragic light resented,
The spirit that is Woman caressed his soul.

Patrick Kavanagh

The moves and moods of Patrick Kavanagh's poetry maintained certain constants. One of these was a sense of "grace in ordinarie". That grace could be explicitly divine and the 'ordinarie' could often be feminine. This poem combines these two ideas in ways anticipatory of today's feminist theology and its prayer-accompaniments.

Prayer

God be praised for the women I have known whose very existence were a praise of you, and yet a demand from you. In their strength and in their gentleness, in their demanding and in their yielding, in their life-giving and their living, in their judging and in their forgiving, they have continued to make you present to me. In your book of life and love I pray that I may read the names inscribed in faulty ways on my aging heart, recorded in my fitful memory. With all of them may you be blessed for ever and ever.

Buíochas/Gratitude

Mithid dom mo bhuíochas
A ghabháil libh, a dhúile,
An comhar a dhíol libh,
A chreaga loma,
A fharraigí cháite,
A chuireadh deocha
Go lách faoi mo ghruanna,
Nuair nach mbíodh cara cáis agam
A d'fhulaingeodh m'ualach,
Ná a d'osclódh doras an fheasa
Sa dún diamhair do mo fhuascailt,
Is neart na tola dorcha
Ag borradh chugamsa.

                    ❧

It's time I made my gratitude
Known to you, you elements,
That I repaid your help,
You bare crags,
You foaming seas
That used to lave
My cheeks so gently
When I had none to confide in,
None who would bear my burden
And open wisdom's door
Inside the enchanted castle to save me
When the force of the dark will
Surged towards me.

Máirtín Ó Díreáin

Máirtín Ó Díreáin, from the Aran Islands, contributed enormously to the renewal of Irish poetry in this century. He once
described 'the poet's duty' as to make words dance before us: *Is
dualgas don fhile focla a chur ar rince os ár gcomhair.* The dance was
always conscious of the elemental dance of nature so significant
for his native islands. There is the ring of the psalmist to some of
these nature poems.

Prayer
For the bared power of your seas and rocks, O Lord, I give thanks.
Sinister as they can appear, there is an elemental comforting
which I too have so often experienced in my eyes and ears, on my
cheeks and hair. Cut off from human comforting and from you,
conscious of the enmity surrounding me and surging towards me,
only the basics of sea and rock could reach and protect me. It is
time for thanks.

The Evangelist John in the Wilderness

I read the Gospel to the sheep and the lions,
the grass and the stars,
to all who will undertake to rework
the world's consciousness,
so that they could have the chance to remember
that they listened to God
while they were still infants.

Ilya Bukstein
from the Russian: Richard McKane

Peter Levi, Oxford Professor of Poetry, wrote: 'Ilya Bukstein is a religious poet in a sense that is somehow impossible in the west, or too full of pitfalls, because it would be too intellectualized; there would be too much taking of an attitude.' The ever 'increasing' opening up of the west to Eastern Europe and its poetry (*cf* Seamus Heaney, *The Government of the Tongue*, 1988) may renew awareness of the religious as well as the political role of poetry and the poet.

Prayer
Let us listen to your Gospel, Lord. To the good news for 'the sheep and the lions, the grass and the stars' let us pay continuous attention. In such an inattentive world, where even the grass and the stars are not safe from earth pollution or star wars, let us become as little children and remember the good news that is ours. For so the beloved disciple and the evangelist of love would have us listen and learn and love.

Hymn to a Broken Marriage

Dear Nessa – Now that our marriage is over
I would like you to know that, if I could put back the clock
Fifteen years to the cold March day of our wedding,
I would wed you again and, if that marriage also broke,
I would wed you yet again and, if it a third time broke,
Wed you again, and again, and again, and again, and again:
If you would have me, which, of course, you would not
For, even you – in spite of your patience and your innocence
(Strange characteristics in an age such as our own) –
Even you require to shake off the addiction of romantic love
And seek, instead, the herbal remedy of a sane affection
In which are mixed in profuse and fair proportion
Loverliness, brotherliness, fatherliness:
A sane man could not espouse a more intimate friend than you.

Paul Durcan

It is very difficult to cope with Paul Durcan's poetry. The bizarre, the utterly irreverent and the insanely sensible crowd and disorientate the reader. The simple lovingness and loveliness of this hymn are almost too touching for public comment.

Prayer
My God, how the breaking bonds entangle us all! The sharp pain of friend and neighbour inhabits our being as their (almost) silent cries penetrate. The fragile unity of man and wife reveals the fragility of all our bonds with one another and with you, our God. This marriage breach is ours also, as friends and lovers, as neighbours and communities. You, O God, had to concentrate us on the 'bridegroom' Jesus before we could 'shake off the addiction of romantic love'. Through your 'patience and innocence' let us be, and be called 'intimate friends'.

Growing Up
from Renoir's drawing: 'Girlhood'

Their two heads, hatted, bowed, mooning
above their waist-high tides of hair
pair hopes.
       This is the haul and full
of fantasy:
       full-skirted girls,
a canvas blued and empty with the view
of unschemed space and the anaemic
quick of the pencil picking out
dreams blooding them with womanhood.

They face the future. If they only knew!

There in the distance, bonnetted,
round as the hairline of a child –
indefinite and infinite with hope –
is the horizon, is the past and all
they look forward to is memory.

Eavan Boland

Poet of private, domestic feelings and events in so many of her poems, Eavan Boland allows us to share the pleasure and the pain from which men in particular may be excluded and to which they are too often indifferent.

We forget so easily that growing up should be an exciting prospect and such an exhilarating experience. To become human minute by minute, inch by inch and love by love is the Creator's gift and call. Girls in bloom are their perfect parable. And Renoir, artist-creator, knew exactly how to present it. The joy in the painting and in the viewing was heralded in Genesis as God looked on creation and saw that it was good.

Prayer

As you looked on your creation, Lord, and saw that it was good, did you also see the shadows, our nightmares as well as our dreams? On that horizon, as earth was formed with darkness and light separated, did original hope already anticipate the future pain? Was the past present? And hopeful dream tinged with regretful memory? That you may not repent of your creation but may leave us 'still infinite with hope', we pray to you, Lord.

Annunciation
From: La Corona

Salvation to all that will is nigh;
That All, which alwayes is All every where,
Which cannot sinne, and yet all sinnes must beare,
Which cannot die, yet cannot chuse but die,
Loe, faithfull Virgin, yeelds himselfe to lye
In prison, in thy wombe; and though he there
Can take no sinne, nor thou give, yet he'will weare
Taken from thence, flesh, which deaths force may trie.
Ere by the spheares time was created, thou
Wast in his minde, who is thy Sonne, and Brother;
Whom thou conceiv'st, conceiv'd; yea thou art now
Thy Makers maker, and thy Fathers mother;
Thou' hast light in darke; and shutst in little roome,
Immensity cloystered in thy deare wombe.

John Donne (1578–1631)

Much of John Donne is already so prayerful in form and content that we scarcely need to move to meditation. This sonnet, the second from a sequence of seven, explores the Gospel mysteries.

Prayer

Hail Mary, we can but imitate the angel in greeting you, faith-filled Virgin. It is so hard to focus our minds on 'immensity cloystered in thy deare wombe'. The uncontainable 'yeelds himselfe to lye in prison, in thy wombe'. That is some measure of the mystery of the immortal who chose to die. We struggle to make sense, to hold in faith and turn to the nearest and dearest connection, the woman concerned, the mother. And the mystery mounts. For all our shared humanity, you have become 'Thy Maker's maker, and thy Father's mother' and our pitiful understanding is further compounded. And yet we trust, for the immensity cloistered in your womb was light and life and love.

Suddenly

Suddenly after long silence
he has become voluble.
He addresses me from a myriad
directions with the fluency
of water, the articulateness
of green leaves; and in the genes,
too, the components
of my existence. The rock,
so long speechless, is the library
of his poetry. He sings to me
in the chain-saw, writes
with the surgeon's hand
on the skin's parchment messages
of healing. The weather
is his mind's turbine
driving the earth's bulk round
and around on its remedial
journey. I have no need
to despair; as at
some second Pentecost
of a Gentile, I listen to these things
round me: weeds, stones, instruments,
the machine itself, all
speaking to me in the vernacular
of the purposes of One who is.

R.S. Thomas

For all his frequent bleakness, R.S.Thomas can suddenly discover and brilliantly expose the universal presence of God. This hymn to the universe can easily take hold of tired and dispirited minds and hearts. To those suffering from Christian burn-out it could bring fresh energy and new Pentecostal life.

Prayer

I needed the silence, Lord. I needed it to concentrate my mind, to sharpen my ear, to sensitise my antennae. Then it became depressing, painful. The sudden, unexpected, voluble address from a myriad directions is ear-shattering, mind-displacing but burden-removing. The blessed relief of communication, of the divine artist's self-expression in swelling tide and whispering leaf! My own body joins the chorus, the chorus of the rock, of the God whose articulate fidelity and loving kindness are rock-persistent and surgeon-delicate. Caught in the whirlwind of your spirit, spinning our planet through cycles of life, I share the morning freshness of Genesis and Pentecost. I observe all that is good and so of you, my God. I organise the rich choir of creative voices into my limited range of language and music to praise you still.

Praying

As lark ascending
Ending in air
Sings its song there
If sounds I am sending
Don't go anywhere
I seem not to care.

After singing the lark
Drops back to the ground
I cover the dark
With the palm of my hand
As horses in fields suddenly stop
Their gallop at a horizon and crop.

P.J. Kavanagh

This image of prayer as sheer song conveys a marvellous sense of prayer's useless beauty and of the subject's detachment from self-seeking. The return to earth invokes the sinister tones of dark and death only to yield to ordinary renewed life in horses cropping.

Prayer
Let us surrender to the movement of this poem, O God, and ask, 'Is it praying or dying?' The lark's ascent, I mean. Have I too the freedom to let go of the sounds I am sending and then 'not to care'?

For that liberation of lark and poet, I too pray, God, but when I drop back to the ground what shall I do with the 'dark'? Let the palm of your hand cover my darkness. Too often have I galloped at horizons that didn't recede but awaited me in all their ghastly stage-set pretentiousness. Horses refuse that temptation. Finally they stop, lower their heads and crop. For such grace and judgement I still beseech you, Lord.

PART THREE

Meditation: *Places Apart*

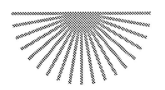

Between Heaven and Bekan Cross

'Home is where one starts from.' And home was Bekan. Outsiders found the name strange, comical rather, especially as we pronounced it B-A-C-O-N just as we insisted on spelling it for them as B-E-K-A-N. Beckon, particularly with Cross, was the best they could manage. The cross (roads) was not central to Bekan but marked its boundaries with the neighbouring villages of Treenreevagh and Liosanuisge. Down the road from the Cross lay the northern boundaries of Spotfield or, for the more informed and more occidental, Brackloon and Brackloon West. In between these confining boundaries was the secular and sacred centre of Bekan vill- age and parish, with parish church, parish house, school and shop. Along that strip of sand road between Brackloon and Liosanuisge I was born and grew up, a quintessential Bekan man.

Beyond the boundaries

The physical boundaries of Bekan were narrow. Brickens and Logboy to the south, with their own churches and schools, and Larganboy to the north with its schools, seemed at times as remote as London or even Peking. We had little reason and very little means to go there in the 'thirties and early 'forties. Yet our mental boundaries circled the globe. The harsh realities of emigration made Birmingham and Boston our neighbours, home for aunts and uncles, brothers and sisters. A missionary and sometimes just a wandering spirit took us and our families through Africa, Asia, San Francisco and Sacramento to Chicago and New York. For all our village voices we quickly acquired the travellers' ranging minds which made it all the more surprising to us to meet later so many people with imperial voices and village minds

We were the travelling people of the time. Of about twenty boys in the national school sixth class of 1943, perhaps one is in Bekan and three or four in Ireland. Our predecessors had left before us and so did most of our immediate successors. The thirties and forties and fifties were hungry times around Bekan Cross and people went where the work and food were. Yet there was vitality and enjoyment at football and sports, at plays, feises, dancing, visiting and even the odd house-ball. The plays are my sharpest memory, held in the local school and, through the thirties and early forties, directed to raising money for the new church.

Celebration

Football, sports, perch fishing in Eaton's Lake, rabbit hunting with snares and then with ferrets and nets took us through 'parables of sunlight' every summer Sunday, a festival of light as likely to occur in January as in July. That unpredictable weather could be as disappointing to 'green and carefree' boys as to care-worn farmers looking anxiously through the rain at the hay lying 'along the side-face of the hill'. Unpredictability worked both ways. We boys felt sometimes that we were having it both ways, splashing through August puddles or escaping early from school to slide on Tarpey's pond, fresh frozen. Every weather turn-around was a new opportunity even when it washed out feis or football.

The mobile authority on weather and a wider world was Willie, postman, sacristan and still full of the wonders of war in the Dardanelles. His authority was increased by the possession of an early wireless. His explanation on his postal rounds of the latest weather situation was classically rendered as 'Willie's auntie is cycling over in France and the weather won't improve until she comes back here.' The Christmas post, with the critical registered letters from Birmingham and Boston, took longer and longer to deliver each day. The refuelling in the houses at the end of the lane took increasing time and the last stage of the day's journey suggested a more difficult relationship between Willie and his bike.

The occasional Christmas difficulties with the bike which Willie experienced should not be misinterpreted. Opportunities of that kind and funds to avail of them were few enough for adult males in those times. In later Munich student-days I was asked about inter-church activity in my home parish and had to confess: 'In my home parish when I was growing up we hadn't a Protestant, a policeman or a public house!' The last privation was naturally the most shocking to Bavarian beer-lovers and could create an extra obstacle to ecumenical dialogue. Dialogue of a most ecumenical kind went on at card games and visiting sessions, although it mostly lacked a partner from a different christian tradition. The visit home of the occasional Bekan girl with an English Protestant from Kilburn or Kidlington, proved no particular problem to our religious traditions. Our generally latent ecumenism was no doubt due to the absence of present threat or resentful memory of Protestant overlords.

Emigration

In so much of this, poverty was protection. The land was poor and other openings for employment and wealth scarcely existed. There was no pub at all through my early years, presumably because people lacked the capital and the prospects among the customers Bekan could provide. Poverty was protection and privation for the few who stayed. The comely maidens and active youth left the locality to the primary school children and the elderly. Funerals were the great social events. Weddings and baptisms too few to make much impact. There were the truly sad funerals of the young and of the not-so-young with young families to be reared.

But mostly the funerals were of those ripe with years who slid slowly away from us and occasioned a coming together of family and neighbours that was rich and even joyful despite the background of death and bereavement. A strong, but seldom simple, faith could put such deaths in perspective and allow for the celebration of rare reunion, all the more poignant because the 'dying' of total emigration to the accompaniment of an 'American wake' are at the horizon of my memory. I am not sure whether I remember the wakes themselves or other people recounting and remembering them. I do remember the lonely scenes at local railway stations as my contemporaries and their predecessors set off for the first time to Manchester and Birmingham and London. The green and carefree boys and their sisters were leaving their Bekan home to find work and house in England.

England was another country but with the going and coming, mostly the going in those years, not so strange and not so far away. Everywhere else, with the possible exception of America, was 'out foreign'. Our main representatives 'out foreign' were missionary priests, brothers and sisters. My days in Munich were locally described as 'being out foreign' in ways a son or daughter in Birmingham or Boston would not be.

Bekan in transition

Changes came, easing and enriching the life. The ESB and

the 'tar' and the pump brought fresh light and mobility and life. Secondary and vocational schools for boys and girls ensured better preparation for the job market. Still they went. The job market hadn't got that far west as yet. Now they frequently stopped off in Dublin and never saw the mailboat until they went to meet the elder brothers and sisters, uncles and aunts coming home for holidays. The employment 'Pale' was pushed gradually and partially west. Bekan with Ballyhaunis, Claremorris and Knock(its three satellite towns) began to enjoy the sixties boom. Television became standard houshold equipment. The EEC membership transformed small farming. Bekan was changing rapidly and, once I lost my parents, I was losing touch.

Return for Sunday Mass is still a moving experience. The faces I recognise are grown older like my own or have appeared in the fresh incarnations of a new generation. Celebrating the fiftieth anniversary of the church in which I made my first confession and first communion, was confirmed and offered my first Mass was particularly affecting. I was baptised in the old church next (bricked-up) door. Adapting the words of W.B. Yeats I knew 'My country is still Bekan Cross'.

Maynooth Matters

'Thank God for McCarthy.' Thus J.G. McGarry remarked as he came through the archway into St Joseph's Square sometime in the 1960s and glimpsed the May sun on the college chapel and spire. Pugin's student who designed the chapel, built for Maynooth's first centenary, conveyed a lightness and joy which, for McGarry at least, the more imposing work of the master in the adjoining St Patrick's missed. Not everybody appreciated the lightness and joy. Sean O'Casey thought of the spire as piercing the heart of Ireland. First year science students in 1948 waded through tons of pigeon droppings to do their barometric readings for a simple height experiment. Yet the spire was to generations of students, in an important and symbolic way, inspiring. And it dominated in different forms the cover of their most sustained and substantial publication, *The Silhouette*.

What kind of symbol should we look for at the end of Maynooth's second centenary? The renewal of the Pugin and McCarthy buildings betokens fidelity to Maynooth's inheritance, which forms the essential basis for all authentic renewal, material and spiritual. For a Maynooth and an Irish Church facing such a changed and changing Ireland and world, the fidelity of Maynooth has to be creative. (Marcel, with his *fidélité creatrice*, was once a student cult-figure.) How will fidelity and creativity find expression in Maynooth's spiritual and pastoral training?

Spirituality as faith-hope-love alive

Spirituality has always been a tricky word in the Maynooth vocabulary. There were of course spiritual fathers with spiritual direction for the presumed spiritual life of each student of the seminary. It was all a little embarrassing to discuss, often for very healthy reasons. Many Irish clergy rejoiced in a hard-headed attitude to more banal devotions. The local paper headline on reported visions in the area, 'Parish Priest keeping an Open Mind', was taken to mean that he didn't believe a word of it. That kind of

scepticism would not be uncommon and showed the crude edge of
the common-sense spirituality of Maynooth men. There was a great
deal more to it and a great deal more may be needed in the future.
At least what has been there and valuable needs more explicit expression and discussion despite a further traditional Maynooth
hesitancy about the value of parading one's deeper concerns or
even putting words on them. In a culture which is no longer pre-
dominantly home-produced and in which the currency of human
communication is dominantly secular, there is a need to name,
discuss and develop these hidden aspects of priestly and indeed
christian faith, hope and love.

What spirituality is fundamentally about is the personal
communal living of faith-hope-love. To write them in such linked
fashion is to emphasise their unity in bible, liturgy and living. It
would also be useful to adapt the traditional definition of theology by Saint Anselm to 'faith-hope-love seeking understanding'.
This would more easily connect the spiritual life and theology, a
connection often felt to be missing by students and priests. It
would also dissipate some of the confusion in the current debate
about the primacy of theory or praxis in theology and about the
primacy of orthodoxy or orthopraxis, as criterion of truth.
Faith-hope-love in dynamic unity form the heart of christian
living or spirituality and the basis for christian reflection or
theology.

Masters of spirituality and theology over the centuries have
emphasised the basic common character of christian living. From
St Paul to Karl Rahner (cf. *Theological Investigations*, vol. 19, pp.
17-138) faith-hope-love derive from and incorporate into the
life, death and resurrection of Jesus Christ. And this is so for all
christians, from primary school pupil to pope. For the priest, the
ordained minister, the grace and task of spirituality are first of
all shared with the whole christian community. What they are giv-
en and called to be is what the priest is given and called to be. In
his role as community leader he is empowered and required to develop his faith-hope-love with and for the others. To neglect this
basic requirement is to neglect his central christian and priestly
task. Without the witness of a vibrant faith-hope-love in his own
life, his proclamation of Word and celebration of Sacrament will
be exposed to contradiction.

This is all so very obvious. Yet much talk of priestly
spirituality or of a special spirituality for the diocesan priest

may ignore it or at least assume it too easily. Return to basics is a
constant task, nowhere more constantly tasking than in christian
living and development. In the traditional pre-1966 Maynooth,
there were many reminders of that need to return, to turn again, in
shub and *metanoia, conversio*, and penance. Conversion as a continuing process expresses permanent renewal and growth required in
christian and spiritual life.

The new Maynooth provides a sharper, more concrete
reminder of the shared spirituality of all christians in the
presence of lay students and staff. The priest who is to share in
spiritual growth with his people has now, as student, opportunity
to share in liturgy and informal prayer, in theological reflection
and social engagement with lay contemporaries. This may not be
yet as formally and explicitly developed as it might. There has
been a natural desire to preserve and promote much of the old
seminary spirit of prayer and quiet, of communal life and
personal discipline. Yet a great deal of informal challenge and
support in faith-hope-love is inevitable. A woman-president of
the John Paul II Theology Society and a black woman leading the
B.D., both in the academic year 1986-87, reveal a significant
aspect of changing relationships in the study of theology. The
theology cannot and certainly should not be divided from the
spirituality. Each year at the Pontifical Degree Mass and later
ceremony of conferring, the deeper connections in shared faith-
hope-love are manifested. These connections and relationships
must over the years enrich both groups, priests and laypeople, and
facilitate the more explicit, named spiritual development which
parishes and parishioners increasingly need.

A school of prayer

It sounds un-Maynooth-like to think of a university-
seminary, and still more of a parish, as a school of prayer. Yet that
must be a primary characteristic of both, a characteristic that
will of course be heavily dependent on the mediative rigour of
good theology. As more people seek a personal faith-hope-love, a
personal prayer life, priests as liturgical and faith leaders will be
more and more called on to initiate and promote prayer-schools
of formal and informal kinds. The range of prayer gifts and needs
in any parish far exceed the capacity of any one priest or even
groups of priests. And in any event parish prayer-schools, while
they will need inspiration and leadership from their priests, can

and should produce many of their own teachers. Indeed a prayer-school in this full christian tradition ought to be a kind of spiritual commune or kibbutz in which, as far as possible under the power of the Holy Spirit, the gifts of all are utilised and the needs of all are met. The present Maynooth context could anticipate, test and promote such developments.

The specifics of priestly spirituality, which distinguish it from generic christian spirituality, relate to office and ministry. It could be called a pastoral spirituality, at least as far as the priest in the parish is concerned. It is more convenient than to include pastoral spirituality, the specific shaping of christian faith-hope-love by pastoral ministry, in the discussion of pastoral ministry.

Pastoral ministry and a ministerial church

Pastoral office and preparation for it have always been central to Maynooth's task. However, pastoral training in terms of acquiring developed pastoral skills and experience as well as theological reflection on such experience did not, apart from previous exercises in preaching and administering the sacraments, receive that much explicit attention in student courses up to quite recently. Course stress was on acquiring a solid grasp of theology. The apprenticeship came later, after ordination, and the skills could be picked up on the job. It would be silly to ignore the substantial successes of that training in the past. Whatever may be said of its express theological creativity, Catholicism Irish style was remarkably successful pastorally through much of the last and well into this century, not only in Ireland but throughout the English-speaking world. The Maynooth model played a critical role in that success.

The different times in which Irish priests must now work require fresh attitudes, new skills and the ability to theologise on the job. In Maynooth as elsewhere moves have been made to meet the challenge. Yet it has to be acknowledged that pastoral training and experience with the necessary faith reflection remain marginal to the programme for most of the three years' theology leading to degree or diploma. Priestly training has not yet moved significantly towards the mix of theory and practice which has characterised medical training, for example, for so long.

The new enlarged lay-setting at Maynooth could stimulate useful developments in pastoral training. More important may be

Maynooth's closer contact with the various Irish dioceses who must in the end provide the immediate pastoral training for students today as it did for young priests in the past. Exchange with dioceses abroad now operates at student level with quite a number of German and other European students taking part or all of their course at Maynooth and Maynooth students getting pastoral experience in Britain and elsewhere.

The international dimension of Maynooth is not of course just European and has naturally developed with ease of travel and communications. This has restored to Maynooth some of its historic missionary links. Columban (Maynooth Mission to China) and Kiltegan (St Patrick's Missionary Society) students, as well as students from the other influential missionary congregations like SMA, SVD and SDB, help provide a fresh missionary vision for diocesan students. That the whole church is missionary, and that African or Latin American missions to Ireland may be as important as Irish missions to Africa and Latin America, are important givens in the training of all future Maynooth priests. Pastoral horizons are suddenly extended and the value of basic christian communities and of other overseas pastoral initiatives can be discussed and assessed on a more informed and sympathetic basis. The praxis and experience which some missionary students acquire in their student years stimulate students and staff at home and suggest parallel experiments in the home dioceses. Students might even interrupt their academic careers with pastoral assignments or return after a couple of years for theological reflection.

Team work

One of the crucial features of ministry and of training for ministry now and in the future must be team work. The individual, of the most diverse talents and abundant energy, can no longer hope to meet the varied demands each ministerial day brings. Ministry operates in a communal setting and with a collegial character. The presbyterate in any diocese is to operate precisely in this way, not for pragmatic reasons of efficiency and specialisation, but for theological reasons, reasons of faith-hope-love. Indeed it may be said that, as a christian community is by grace and vocation a caring community, it is also a ministering and ministerial community.

In his representative work of preaching this gospel, celebrating the eucharist and building the christian community, the priest acts with and out of community. He acts to enable the community to act, to accept, understand and proclaim in its turn the good news of salvation; to celebrate and worship by remembering the death of the Lord and sharing his body and blood; to share with and care for one another and so witness to how christians love one another. These activities must have, as far as possible, a collegial shape. In the parish that collegial shape will involve priests, religious and laity in formal and informal patterns. Lay readers and lay eucharistic ministers offer one formal and liturgical example of that. Such collegiality cannot stop at the church door any more than the priest's ministerial and pastoral activity can. The slowly emerging ideal pattern suggests a partnership in ministry which gradually embraces the whole parish, diocese and larger christian community (cf. Enda Lyons, *Partnership in Parish*). As each christian accepts responsibility in and for the christian community, it becomes a genuinely caring and ministering community. Such a community becomes an effective sign of the inbreaking Kingdom of God. It points the way to the emergence of a wider society, in Ireland and elsewhere, in which the Kingdom values of freedom, justice and peace find fuller expression.

Maynooth has an important place in Ireland's partnership ministry and in preparing students for it. Within the college itself, diverse constituencies of staff and students have the opportunity for mutual ministry. Clerical and lay, diocesan, missionary and religious students can collaborate in truly ministerial and enriching fashion. Similar interaction and collaboration between college as a ministerial centre and the dioceses, the missionary and religious congregations, can offer stimulus and guidance, experience and reflection in pastoral ministry. The priest is no longer expected to operate simply as an isolated pastor. With his priestly colleagues and the embryonic pastoral team which many parishes now enjoy, he may hope to enable christian people to build christian community. The pastoral spirituality of such a pastoral servant and enabler will give a specific shape to the more general christian spirituality.

Some immediate problems

The exciting prospects in prayer and pastoral ministry, which are opening up for the Church, require more thoughtful preparation by seminary and diocese. And some immediate special Irish needs should be noted here. A partnership spirituality and ministry will have to pay special attention to the poor, the deprived and the excluded. A caring, ministering community is distinguished by its concern for these. In contemporary Ireland the poor in the economic sense is a large and growing section of the population, particularly through unemployment. Their economic privation is reinforced by increasing powerlessness, exclusion from decision-making which then bears even harder on them. Priestly leadership is a critical christian requirement just now. The idealism of Maynooth students has to be helped to find adequate expression in their relations with the poor.

A related experience of exclusion, in society and particularly in church, is reported by many Irish women. Ecomonically poor women carry a double burden. In the current Maynooth, clerical students have to work with young women in a variety of contexts, including theology. This could prove useful in developing a ministering community in which women find proper outlet for their ideals and ideas. Without women's participation, the Church's ministry is inevitably less caring and seriously incomplete.

In this unsystematic listing of immediate demands on Church and ministry, the challenge of interchurch relations may not be ignored. So much as been done in twenty years and so much remains to be done. At Maynooth there has been a procession of distinguished lecturers from other churches, such as John Macquarrie, James Haire, Thomas Torrance and Wolfhart Pannenberg. Maynooth students attend interchurch conferences and invite students from other churches to Maynooth. Yet in face of Northern Irish violence and western world secularism, more urgent and continuous cooperation is necessary. Already some Irish Protestant students have graduated at Maynooth. An Orthodox priest from Romania was awarded his doctorate in June 1987. Perhaps the time is approaching for more formal and extensive exchange where some Maynooth students might spend a month with Presbyterian, Methodist and Church of Ireland students and some of them might spend a month at Maynooth. Such experience of the spiritual and theologial ethos of the others could provide a basis for deeper ecumenical understanding and continuing pastoral collaboration.

Maynooth is kept alive by new generations. New generations, in the famous phrase of John Paul II, are new continents. The new generations of students for the priesthood who will have to minister in word and sacrament and pastoral care to Irish generations yet unborn, have an exciting yet daunting prospect. What has been accomplished in Maynooth will, we pray, stimulate their creative fidelity in ways that have connections with the hints and guesses thrown out here. Faithful to the future, under the power of the Spirit, must characterise Maynooth and the Irish Church now as it did two hundred years ago.

The college spire still stands clear. Nearby the elegant new library negotiates between the Pugin-McCarthy buildings and the future. Opposite sits Imogen Stuart's strong bronze of John Paul II embracing the new generations. Symbols for the future Maynooth are emerging.

The Blessingbourne Initiative

On the Golden Jubilee of the foundation, by Hugh Montgomery, of The Irish Association for Cultural, Economic, and Social Relations

Some philosophers maintain that need is a more fundamental moral drive than love. And whatever need drove Major General Hugh Montgomery and his colleagues together in 1938, it certainly has not diminished by 1988. The points of contact between peoples north and south have significantly increased and intensified. Organisations and institutions like Cooperation North, Glencree, Corrymeela, the Social Studies Conference, and a range of others have in the last few decades struggled, sometimes hopefully, sometimes despairingly, to promote communication and cooperation in innumerable imaginative ways. 'And the sea rises higher yet.' From Enniskillen to Gibraltar to the Falls Road, through the byroads of Northern Ireland and the highways of Europe, Irish and British offer bloody and unmistakeable signals of the divisive and often murderous hostility that still exists in this island, between these islands and in the European Community itself. What we are faced with now is not simply the hostile division of Irish people, or of Irish and British peoples, but of Europeans. The shadows of our divide reach Holland and Germany, just as they and we seek to proclaim the deeper unity of Europe.

The European paradox is instructive. Beginning with the economic, and confined at first to a small range of such issues between a small group of countries, the Benelux countries, the Europe of six and of the Treaty of Rome gradually grew to ten and then twelve, primarily on the basis of economic interest. The cultural interchange and mutual enrichment have followed – much too slowly for some of us, but yet steadily. Political developments at the intergovernmental level have been crucial but partial, with the next step to greater political coherence and representativeness uncertain and debatable. Yet the twin engines of growing political trust and evident economic need have brought the traditional enemies of Western Europe to this impressive stage of mutual respect and cooperation only forty years after the most destructive war in the history of the world. Mutual and national self-interest reinforced each other, from the centre of Europe to its margins, even if they have still a long way to go before traditional hostilities and destructive rivalries finally disappear. These islands can contribute to that development but they can and do also obstruct it, not least in their own internal relations, which are becoming, as never before, European relations.

This is not a proposal to make the Irish Association for Cultural, Economic and Social Relations into the European Association for same, as if, after fifty years of futile effort within this misty island, we sought refuge in the sun cities of Europe. No such escape is proper or possible. But, looking to life beyond the Irish Association's Golden Jubilee Celebrations, it is essential to recognise the differences between 1938 and 1988. 1938, year of Munich and the surrender of Czechoslavakia, year of the Kristallnach, a year ominous with the impending destruction of Europe, was also the year of the Blessingbourne Initiative. Lest Blessingbourne appear trivial, Paddy Kavanagh's ghost comes whisperin

> I have lived in important places, times
> When great events were decided, who owned
> That half a rood of rock, a no-man's land
> Surrounded by our pitchfork-armed claims.
> I heard the Duffys shouting 'Damn your soul'
> And old McCabe stripped to the waist, seen
> Step the plot defying blue cast steel –
> 'Here is the march along these iron stones'
> That was the year of the Munich bother. Which
> Was more important? I inclined
> To lose my faith in Ballyrush and Gortin
> Till Homer's ghost came whispering to my mind.
> He said: 'I made the Iliad from such
> a local row. Gods make their own importance.'

And lest we forget Blessingbourne, lest Irish people forget how much they share in geography and history, in recent and remote ethnic and cultural background, in endured and mutually inflicted suffering, a small group from north and south established a forum, a platform, a channel of continuous communication on these deeper and more urgent issues, deeper and more urgent than particular constitutional arrangements, the cultural, the social and the economic issues. Division and war and suffering did not prevent, and may have inspired these brave few to transcend traditional divisions and traditional political and religious pre-occupations.

Similar evils, but on an altogether vaster scale, inspired the Schumanns and the Monnets to transcend Europe's traditional hostilities and political preoccupations in promoting community and cooperation in the economic, social and cultural areas. As we are not seeking to become a European Association, neither are we seeking to pursue any particular political policy. Our political strategy and strength must be to continue as the impartial forum for all the genuinely political parties and protagonists in the island. Indeed, despite our fuller title, much of our work, and that our best work, in the last twenty years, has been providing platforms and fora for politicians who would otherwise have little public or indeed private opportunity to communicate. The May 1988 seminar on the Review of the Anglo-Irish Agreement, with politicians north and south, is a particularly stimulating example of this. Its highlight was the courteous, rational yet forceful exchange between Ken Magennis, Official Unionist MP, and Seamus Mallon of the SDLP. Such possibilities for politicians, and for the participation of a wider public with them, are still too rare.

Politicians in Ireland, particularly perhaps in Northern Ireland, but across the world also, can be captive to an electorate that is uninformed and unwilling to be informed. Only an increasingly aware public can set politicians free to think and act beyond the inherited boundaries of prejudice and blindness, and so serve the real interests of the prejudiced and the blind. The beautiful blindness of the Frank McGuinness character in 'Carthaginians' – 'But Catholics can't be bigots' – raises the inevitable laugh from the audience. The more tragic dimension lurks there for all, Catholics and Protestants, southerners and northerners.

The Irish Association, no longer on its own but in goodly company, seeks to remove that blindness and deafness and prejudice we have towards one another on this island. These are no doubt in part wilful, or at least become wilful when we refuse to

examine them. John Hewitt's 'Coasters' captures the indifference
of too many for too long

> You coasted along
> to larger houses, gadgets, more machines,
> to golf and weekend bungalows,
> caravans when the children were small,
> the Mediterranean, later, with the wife.
> You even had a friend or two of the other sort,
> coasting too: your ways ran parallel.
> You coasted along
> And all the time, though you never noticed,
> the old lies festered;
> Now the fever is high and raging;
> but who would have guessed it, coasting along?
> You coasted too long.

The prejudice and destruction have immediate political or
religous-political origins. Overcoming them requires a broader
vision, more and better channels of communication, more frequent and more creative encounters with the others. In business and
the professions a great deal of useful meeting between north and
south, unionists and nationalists, undoubtedly occurs. It has often
survived and thrived by its very quietness and above all by avoiding
the crunch issues, political and religious differences. This has
also been true of so many family gatherings, neighbourhood
groups, amateur organisations, holiday encounters. That these
meetings continue to take place is desperately important. More
is now called for. Not acrimonious political debate, not an agonising search for immediate solutions, but at least the voicing of
our need to know and understand one another, beyond the business
or professional or personal contact. To know and understand each
other in our history and culture, in our social triumphs and failures as different yet related peoples, in our unionist or nationalist affiliation. Above all we need to know and understand one another in our need for a peaceful and just community. Politicians
cannot deliver without our cooperation and communication.
Whatever the future political structures of this island, of these
islands, of Western Europe, the peoples of this island must get to
know, understand, accept and finally cherish one another, if our
children and their children are to have a life worth living. Every-

body here has that role and responsibility to promote communication, cooperation and so community.

Politics may be finally unavoidable but it is not everything. Our 'Celebration of Ulster' moved away very deliberately from politics and politicians, important as they are. The creative achievements of Ulster people in recent decades has been astonishing. To give millennial Dublin a taste of this was our ambition. The exhibitions, the plays, the concerts, the poetry readings are all powerful witness to that creative life-force which must surely triumph over the dead hand of Ulster. To us in the south, to join with the life-forces and the creativity of the north is an urgent call. As the conversation must extend beyond the politicians, so must it extend beyond politics.

More areas of communication, more communicators within and without the Irish Association, these are our needs. And what of the more obviously suffering, deprived and neglected who would have great difficulty with the manners, accents and even the vocabulary of the Irish Association? How do we reach them?

W. B. Yeats reminded us very forcibly of the dilemma of liberals and of revolutionaries: 'When the beggars have changed places but the lash goes on', or again in 'Parnell': 'Parnell came down the road, he said to a cheering man: Ireland shall get her freedom and you still break stone?'

In so much of modern Ireland, north and south, there are no stones to break, only lives and minds and hearts. In the clash of ideologies and ideologues, of armies in the Irish night, the'coasters' are mainly protected, while the unemployed and the impoverished, and still more the women and children among them, are the more vulnerable and suffer the more. In the communication between Irish people that leads to fuller community, the unemployed of east and west Belfast, of Dublin and Derry, of Enniskillen and Enniscorthy, must be enabled to participate.

A community, participatory and inclusive Ireland, with whatever political structures, has more obstacles to overcome than that of nationalist and unionist, Catholic and Protestant. The excluded are all about us. An Irish Association for cultural, social and economic affairs must seek to include in its affairs, those most excluded in our cultural, social and economic power structures.

For that, we need as members vigorous, competent, compassionate people who can recognise the excluded and the hostile as the potential neighbour. That commitment to a community, participatory, egalitarian country, beyond political division and inherited prejudice, is a challenge to a generation which might feel we had deserted or betrayed them in our financial, professional success or in our social and political failure. Before they leave for New York or Dusseldorf, they might see the possibilities of Blessingbourne, in ways we never have or could. They might manage to transcend nationalist and unionist mythology and remain Irish in Ireland.

If they do, they could transform this island into a source of Irish and British and European vitality and civilisation of the kind Kenneth Clark saw emerging from the islands of Skellig and Iona in the seventh and eighth centuries. To translate such traditions into life-giving rather than death-dealing forces can often seem impossible. It happened in Ireland and Europe before. It can happen again and in our lifetime.

The jubilees and centenaries and memorials are upon us. 1688, 1789, 1798, 1938, 1968 – orange and green, tricolour and Union Jack, blood and sand. We Europeans all have a savage and creative heritage. In this off-shore island, let the creative heritage prove its value more and more. With our nearest neighbours, let us emulate the reconciliation that has been the most glorious achievement of age-old enemies on mainland Europe. In that advance beyond the boundaries of politics and religion, of sex and class, may the Irish Association continue to play a significant role in promoting a community island – that is, participatory, egalitarian and inclusive.

An Island that Works

Irish people have many reasons to be modest in their immediate ambitions for the economic, political and even religious life of the island. Wealthy and poor, nationalists and unionist, Catholic and Protestant are deeply locked into divisions which are destructive of community and preventive of progress. As disciples of the Jesus Christ who transcends and overcomes all divisions, we believe that the resources of his word and sacrament must be recovered by Irish people in pursuit, not of any grandiose return of the island of saints and scholars, but of the much more modest aim, an island that works.

Repentance and shared suffering
Although Jesus initiates his ministry in the Gospels with the call to penance, most christians find it difficult to apply this to themselves in times of crisis. This is particularly true of people with power, leaders in church or state, in industry or agriculture. The acknowledgement of precise failures and of continuing self-centredness, which the Catholic sacrament of penance is so rightly insistent on, is readily rationalised as inappropriate or even impossible for institutions and their leaders. As if institutions and their leaders were incapable of grievous errors and self-centredness and as if these grievous errors could be corrected and atoned for without acknowledgement. The complicity of the churches as institutions in the continuing failure to make this island work, and their consequent summons to penance, acknowledgement and conversion, might seem so clear and urgent as to be taken for granted by all. Yet the old unrepentant tones may still be heard. The call to conversion is always applied to the others.

At least the suffering, the destructive consequences of the divisions, is more evenly spread over Catholic and Protestant, nationalist and unionist, if not evenly over rich and poor men and women. There is always an underclass in what may appear the most widely shared suffering. Women, the poor and above all poor women, form the regular underclass in any suffering society. As the underclass bear the heavier burdens and have the least resources in coping with them, the inevitable upper class, including the institutional leaders, have the lighter burdens and the greater resources. Sharing the suffering fairly demands a deliberate choice by protected leaders and upper class, a choice which disciples of Jesus, and more particularly their church leaders, ignore or refuse at the peril of their life and love in Christ.

Entering into the widespread suffering deriving from the bomb and the bullet, from intimidation both crude and subtle, from economic devastation, is a necessary condition for christians living in Ireland today. Where the suffering are, there must be christians with their Master. This is a more profound and effective response to penance than superficial handwringing about failure and guilt. Taking on the suffering in solidarity, in protest and finally in transformation, is the way Jesus Christ has mapped out for those who would come after him. Laying down one's life for one's friends takes the form of sharing their suffering in order to overcome it, to bring them the good news of salvation.

Sharing the suffering derived from Irish divisions is aimed at removing it by gradually and eventually overcoming the divisions. The very sharing is already an overcoming of division. The purification through further shared suffering confronts the leadership and the privileged with the sources of suffering and their need to harness their resources more generously and effectively. The experience of failure which will often be theirs should draw the privileged more deeply into the struggle against destructive division. Suffering cannot be simply wiped away. It must be shared and endured so that if it proves ineradicable, and some human suffering is, people may find, through it and beyond it, human dignity and fulfilment. The illusory belief that all human suffering is removable may not however excuse from the christian call that all human suffering is shareable and in sharing by God and neighbour finally conquerable. In the island that works, shared suffering is a crucial human and christian way forward.

Where the division is deep, as it frequently is in Ireland, and the suffering on both sides acute, christians in attempting to share the suffering on both sides face the risk of rejection by both. The further suffering of christians who would share with the divided sufferers can contribute in its own way to the process of repentance and conversion. In that no-man's-land between warring sides, all christians may discover their crucified vocation. It is there also that they may hope to find the life and love which as grace 'superabounds' (Romans 5).

Working together and New Creation

Sharing the suffering, taking on the chaos, cosmic and man-made, afflicting the island, to which Irish christians are called in company with their God, is by divine intention and example directed to the emergence of a new expression of the reign of God, new creation. Human beings are charged with the glorious responsibility of being co-creators in a universe hovering between chaos and fulfilment. As co-creators they seek with God and with one another to recognise and respect, to harness and transform the God-given earthly and human resources. Work as care for, production and transformation of the goods of the earth, as the service of human community, as the creativity of the human spirit, is the responsibility and right of all to share in the creative activity of God. Beyond shared suffering lies the christian vocation to work and co-create with one another and with God.

In a society where so many are excluded from work, co-creation becomes increasingly an impossibility. The recognised workers, those with jobs, who wish to be authentic co-creators, have to reach beyond their obligation to be honest and effective workers and seek to share with those excluded from the present job structure. They have to encourage and enable the emergence of a collaborative and co-creative society by work-sharing and job creation. Management and unions, entrepreneurs and public servants, employed and unemployed, have to seek to-gether to provide for the structured participation by all adults in the co-creative enterprise of making the island work. Working for oneself is only part of the christian creative vocation. Seeking to expand the work possibilities for others in production and service and refusing to reduce these possibilities for personal advantage are also part of the christian call. An island that works is an island that works to ensure that all have the opportunity, dignity and ful-filment of participating in the development of the island's re-sources and in the service of its people. An island that attempts to work in this fashion may gradually see beyond divisions which issue in the personal suffering and social paralysis so evident at present. Suffering together and working together provide hope of finally and fully living together.

Shared prayer and acceptance of difference

The paradox of christian division is that it emphasises not just the call to unity of John 17, but the deepest foundation of unity in the common confession of Jesus as Lord, and in the common recitation of Our Father. To pray to the Father in the name of Jesus, authentic and distinctive christian prayer, makes a nonsense of our historical separations and divisions. Unless we continually remind ourselves of this in our prayer, it will lose its authenticity and distinctiveness. If we do continually remind ourselves we will feel compelled to seek more and more occasions for explicitly shared prayer, for external communal expression together of prayer. Prayer is often diminished in our attempts at separate expression and destroyed where that separate expression takes on the character of deliberately excluding the others from the company of Our Lord and Our Father.

Unity in Christ as daughters and sons of the Father, which characterises christians and through them all humanity, both respects and relativises differences. Each daughter and son of the Father has unique gifts and is called to unique fulfilment, the completion of differentiation as this particular person. Differentiation is necessary to the bonding of the family of the Father, ultimately the whole human family. Respect for each person's difference and differentiation as well as for the values of the tradition and community by which the person has been formed, is an essential part of the respect for the divine creator and originator of all particular human traditions and communities. The respect must be mutual between different and even opposing traditions and communities. No tradition or community may be elevated to a position which involves disrespect or, still less, contempt and oppression of the other. Traditions and communities elevated in this way become idols, replacement Gods. Their upholders are once again the idolators so prevalent, and so castigated, in Jewish and Christian salvation history. Respect, true respect, for any tradition is relative, always qualified by respect for others and finally subordinate and dependent on respect for the one, true God.

In prayer together, mutual respect and relativisation of all human traditions develop in their foundational setting, recognition of the one creator and saving God. Unionism and nationalism, as political traditions and communities, demand the respect of prayerful christians, but also that essential relativisation which enables unionists and nationalists to go on

being christians. The idolisation of one tradition or the other as
the practical supreme good, one's real God with all the sacrifice
of people and principle which that involves, is a clear denial of
the God of Jesus Christ. Catholicism and Protestantism may well
be similar idols. In the Irish context, they are more likely to be
subordinate, captive idols to rampant nationalism or unionism,
or in a more modern distortion, to a dominant consumerism or
materialism, capitalist or socialist.

Respect and relativisation through prayer, enable people to
maintain the true values of their own community and respect those
of the other. It provides for people's particular identity deriving
from history, while opening them up to the deeper shared identity
of all, deriving from the Lord of history. The human race is today
developing a sense of global identity in search of unity and, indeed, of survival. This is reinforced for christians by their faith in
the one God for all. The Church, in the words of Vatican II, is to
be the sacrament, the sign and (at least partial) realisation of that
unity and community of humankind. Integral to that sacramental
role is the unity of christians themselves. Yet unity may not be the
destruction of, or suppression of difference. Respect for difference in unity is the way of christian love, the holding together of
all the created and creative gifts of God, finally based on the unity
in difference of that true one God. Irish christians have a heavy responsibility in this matter both within their own island and in the
wider world. Responses to the Third World and to the United Na-
tions provide some evidence of their ability to contribute to a
unified world of difference. The more severe test is how far they
can come together as a people on this island to share suffering,
work and prayer while respecting their genuine and valuable
differences. On the basis of the gifts of faith and love which are
certainly theirs for the taking, they have reason to hope for 'an
island that works'.

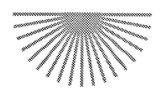

PART FOUR

Preaching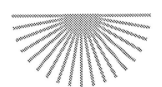

The Risks of Preaching

The aesthetic, ethical and religious risks of preaching developed here might well put prospective preacher or congregation off all further engagement with the sermon. G.K. Chesterton's maxim, 'Whatever is worth doing, is worth doing badly' does not provide adequate reassurance for either preacher or congregation as they suffer through another aesthetically ill-presented, morally self-righteous or religiously trivial sermon. Drawing attention to these widespread risks may be rubbing salt in too many recent wounds. Subsequent examples of preaching are naturally at further risk by being exposed to the critical analysis which precedes them. The physician-preacher may be no better than others at healing the self.

A community exercise

The shift of origin for the sermon from preacher to congregation is not a cheap trick to help evade responsibility. The personal responsibility of the Sunday preacher remains but it includes the responsibility to draw on the resources of the community, their small and large hours of belief, in preparation. His responsibility is in one sense to articulate their faith and their faith-difficulties. He is their spokesperson as well as that of the wiser and older faith-community. And he is called by the Word as preacher to the same conversion to which they are summoned. All the resources of the faith-community are to be marshalled in service of such conversion, a point developed at the end of this section.

The aesthetic risks

The aesthetic risks, the ethical risks and the religious risks of preaching (à la Kierkegaard) would seem a useful classification. By the aesthetic risks I have in mind a number of things. Making sentences is one of our great creative gifts. Yet they demand a form that is at once clear and meaningful and beautiful.

Paragraphs have the same needs. And so to the fuller composition. The form in choice of word, range of associations,
sequence of thought and elegance of structure qualifies effective
mediation between speaker and audience, preacher and congregation. In a world where formlessness may easily destroy verbal communication in grunts and yelps, in ill-formed, unformed and incomplete sentences, where at best informality reduces all modes
to that of the chat-show, preaching provides an opportunity to
preserve and promote a quality of human life in communication
and so community-making. Such preaching should be well formed,
careful of words and caring of people, alert to the beauty of the
message, of its ultimate origin in God and of its final destiny in
human beings.

The beauty of so many languages, including the Irish and English languages, has at high points been reflective of the beauties of
the divine-human interchange in Israel and in Jesus and at the same
time has been greatly enriched by it. Whatever the achievements of
our own civilisations, and they are many and notable, their public
speaking and preaching seldom attain any kind of discernible
beauty.

Preachers are not poets and they should not seek artificially
to 'beautify' their style. Yet they must be stewards both of the
Word and of words. They must seek continuously and imaginatively
to let the Word of God be fittingly formed and properly enfleshed
in the interchange of the weekly sermon or homily. The aesthetic
risk involved in preaching is that its poor practice will contribute
to the further degrading of human speech and so of human life, at
the same time diminishing the saving impact of the Word of God.
Salvation by the Word requires the salvation of the words, their
careful choice and nurturing.

This is no appeal for sheer eloquence, still less sheer
elegance or, worse, some fancy and fanciful self-indulgence in
word-play. Plain-speak may be the most appropriate. Clarity and
directness are always required: the occasion and the audience, the
particular message and preacher, will involve their own particu-
larities of style. Yet style and form, wrought in the mind,
imagination and life of the preacher, are part of his preaching obligation to meet the aesthetic risks to which she or he is exposed.
Preparation in life, reflection and imagination enter into the
forming of the good sermon and such ethical and religious demands influence the aesthetic demands.

The ethical risks

In talking or writing about the risks of preaching one may easily appear to practitioners to overrate the aesthetic risks. It could all seem a bit precious to priests charged with a weekly task. And yet ... However, they may be more open to some discussion of the ethical risks. In some ways these risks are obvious, including risks involving the preacher and risks involving the congregation.

The more obvious and bothersome to some preachers involves both preacher and congregation. That is the risk of being misunderstood. This can have a paralysing effect on some preachers, leading them to stress and repeat some simple, clear and true statement of biblical or church teaching. It can easily end up as platitude which, if not misunderstood by the congregation, does not connect with them at all. And of coure it can easily be mis-understood.

The reality of public communication to audience or congregation involves always multi-understanding. Different aspects of what the preacher or lecturer says in the religious and moral area are picked up by members of the congregation or audience and with different nuances. The same aspect may be given a different emphasis and even understood differently and, still, more, applied differently, by different members of the congregation or audience. This can happen where one is presenting what seems a clear, coherent and systematic account of material to an attentive class with opportunity to study and revise over a whole year, as any recent set of examination scripts testifies. It does not excuse the preacher or lecturer from seeking to be as clear, coherent and accurate as possible. It does mean that he cannot afford to be paralysed into platitude by the fear of misunderstanding.

The reality of multi-understanding implies risk of misunderstanding. Demand for vital communication, presenting living truth as alive, rules out the evasion of platitutde or resort to repetition of lifeless formulae. The teaching of Jesus, its variety of sermon, parable, moral exhortation and paradoxical remark was clearly not risk-free. It is still understood and misunderstood in a host of different ways, and could never, in its multilayered richness, be reduced to a series of abstract, safe formulations. The aesthetic imperative joins with the ethical in summoning the preacher to transcend the platitudinous and formalistic and risk the living, imaginative discourse of which Jesus himself was master.

A less obvious but more penetrating ethical risk for the

preacher is the gap between what he says and what he does. Jesus' criticism of preachers and teachers of his own time fastened on their failure here. The risk can take two opposing forms.

The sensitive preacher may be so conscious of his own limitations as a christian that he may never issue any critical or cutting word of christian truth to his congregation. Awareness of one's own weakness and limitations as christian is admirable and essential to the authentic preacher. It must not however be allowed to prevent or excuse him from speaking the graceful and yet demanding word of God. Authenticity demands acknowledgement of personal limitation, at least indirectly in tone and style. Without such awareness, acknowledgement and acceptance of conversion, a preacher will be gradually exposed as sounding brass and tinkling cymbal.

The other risk of mere words, prophetic and indignant or eloquent as they may sound at first, will have replaced the paralysis of modesty and self-denigration. There is grace for the preacher also if he listens to the words he must speak. If he doesn't, the potential grace for the congregation may easily turn to disillusionment with the words of somebody whose life so clearly contradicts what he says. Short-term disguises may reduce this risk to the congregation. They cannot finally prevent it. The preacher like the teacher is continually giving himself away for good or for ill, for grace or for stumbling-block (*skandalon*).

The religious risks

The religious risks of preaching are inevitably related to the other risks, particularly the ethical risks of being misunderstood, misleading, endorsing the cause of the powerful, and mere verbal posturing, in deep contradiction with the preacher's own lifestyle. Yet the religious risks reach beyond the merely moral or ethical. If the word of God is to be mediated in words genuinely reflective of the divine reality, these words must be an articulation of the preacher's own prayer awareness and prayer struggle. Aesthetics and ethics cannot substitute for the personal in mediating meditation on God's Word which should be basic to every sermon. What joy in the Word, what enjoyment or repose or consolation in God does this preacher express? That could be one crucial question, exposing the risk of religious superficiality.

So could the questions: How far has the preacher struggled with the Word, suffered the cutting edge of its meaning and

applicability in life? Clichéd commonsense commentary or
detached erudite exegesis blunt the cutting edge and empty the
Word of all its saving power. Being bored to spiritual death
proves the greatest risk for too many congregations for all the
efforts and energies of the many vital preachers around.

Personal engagement with the living, challenging Word of
God takes place in a particular social context; familiarity with
that context, indeed immersion in it, is a further necessary requirement of good preaching. Evasion of this context, inability
or unwillingness to analyse and understand it, risks distorting
preaching the Kingdom after the model of Jesus. It becomes at
best an exercise in individualistic spirituality. The goal is restricted to relating 'me and my God'. The communal address to
God, our Father, is ignored. The transformed community to which
the Word of God always summons is obscured. Personal conversion in the true christian model occurs in and for community, in
and through community conversion. The risk of religious individu-
alism encouraged by the best of sermons is still unacceptably high
in our culture.

A serious attempt to overcome that risk demands some communal preparation for preaching. This can and sometimes does
occur as groups of priest-preachers gather regularly to prepare
together the Sunday sermon. This is and should be taken further by
mixed groups of priests, religious and lay people, men and
women, representative of the one people of God. They must struggle together each week to reflect on the Sunday readings in the
context of their actual situation. The preacher in this way is more
fully informed by the Word as it takes flesh in that particular
world. Community preaching and its partner, community
spirituality, must grow out of the community and its struggles to
discern and develop the Kingdom of God among them.

The Cross and the Critical Mind

As I struggled with the making of this sermon, a friend and colleague, graduate of this university, died suddenly. One of the keenest critical minds I had known, he had triumped over a series of strokes in the last four years. In these last years the encounter between the critical mind and the cross, my theme for this reflection, found poignant expression in the physical disability and spirited response of my deceased colleague, Peter Connolly.

The restless, penetrating mind of Paul of Tarsus, with his own fleshly handicap, concentrated on the Cross in what might now be thought an obsessional way. His critical ability and questioning style seemed at the same time to flinch at the prospect of making intellectual sense of what he described as a scandal to the Jews and foolishness to the Greeks (1 Cor 1:23). Calvary's tree of death appeared an insuperable obstacle to dialogue with both Jerusalem and Athens. It has frequently been so. Our own monuments to the power and achievements of the critical mind, such as the university, do not readily accommodate the rough wood and disfigured human body of Christ crucified, all the christian preacher had to offer (1 Cor 1:17).

The good man from Nazareth, even the good teacher – although of course he never published anything, to quote the apocryphal Good Friday table-talk of the Jerusalem dons – might well be given an honorary doctorate or nominated for the Nobel Peace Prize. Such gentle and good people sometimes are. But the criminal on a cross, the religious enthusiast with his courageous claims, announcing a kingdom which he so signally failed to deliver and in whose name so much superstition and exploitation had developed over two thousand years, could withstand very little critical examination. Only the uncritical and the credulous, the dependent and the fearful, could still accept this fringe figure as the key to human existence and human fulfilment. Athens and its sucessors know a good deal better than that.

Yet this Church, this University, this congregation provide

some counter witness. The origins of this and all great European universities in medieval times rested on the conviction that the Cross and the critical mind belong together. It was never an easy alliance. The critical commitment of Thomas Aquinas drew fire from contemporary leaders of the community of the Cross, such as the Archbishop of Paris. The *theologis crucis* of Martin Luther had little appeal for the intellectual humanists of his own or later days. The intervening centuries have undoubtedly produced people of outstanding intellect who took the Cross fully seriously. On this occasion and in this place John Henry Newman comes naturally to mind. Yet the uneasy alliance of medieval and later times has for most university people and institutions all but disintegrated. Even if we do not believe with Nietzsche that Christ 'advanced the process of making men stupid "by placing himself" on the side of the intellectually poor', the study of Jesus' teaching and the significance of his Cross are major intellectual concerns for the very few. Forming critical minds and developing creative spirits go on in university and elsewhere, *etsi Crucifixus non daretur*. 'When', according to Studdart Kennedy's poem, 'Jesus came to Birmingham' and was simply let die, he 'crouched against a wall and cried for Calvary'. It could be any modern city, any modern university.

And yet the Cross is a symbol of truth. For the evangelist, John, Jesus was the truth as well as the way and the life (John 14:6). In his account of the exchange with Pilate it is the sophisticated Roman administrator who evades the critical dimension of truth (John 18:38). In another mood and place, Nietzsche wonders whether 'under the holy fable and travesty of the life of Jesus' there is not hidden 'one of the most painful cases of this martyrdom of knowledge about love' (*Beyond Good and Evil*).

Jesus as martyr to the truth is a valid reading of the Gospel story – in his questioning and challenging of the received opinions and practices of his day, from observance of the Sabbath to dining with harlots and publicans, to preaching a new kingdom and anticipating the destruction of the Temple. The truth that was in him, that took shape in his teaching and ministry was too much for contemporary leaders to bear. To preserve their tradition and, less consciously but more significantly, their position, they had to reject that truth and eventually the truth bearer. The tradition itself should have alerted them to the practice of rejecting the truth by killing the prophets. Among the people of God's own choosings

PREACHING 91

his messengers have always had a hard time. Prophecy, speaking for
God as the ultimate truth, had proved a very costly exercise in the
history of Israel. Jesus' parables and warnings underlined the
lesson of history (cf. Matt 23). Dying for the truth became the
almost inevitable destiny of him who succeeded the prophets to
become the fullness of God's self-communication, last of all his
Son (Matt 21:33 ff; Hebs 1: 1,2). The Word and Truth which had
become flesh did not fit into the system, religious or political.
The doctors in the Temple(Luke 2:46), like those in the first
places in the Synagogue(Mark 12:39), as well as the mighty on
their thrones (Luke 1:52), all felt threatened by the two-edged
sword (Heb 4:12). So it was expedient that this one man of the
disturbing truth should die for the people (John 18:14).

Jesus as the disturbing truth made flesh and made corpse,
remains inspiration and consolation for all the questioning,
critical minds who have to confront the doctors, placemen and
mighty of Church, State and University. In their different ways
these hallowed institutions reflect and provide for some of the
noblest aspirations of human beings, for freedom and justice,
peace and truth; in Gospel terms, Kingdom values all. In their
historical practice all these institutions and their leaders fail
critically.

Central to that failure is surrender to the demonic
temptation of power, so dramatically presented to Jesus in the
Gospels (Matt 4:1-11). The first enemy of that power is truth,
passion of the questioning, challenging, critical mind. In truth
shall we be saved from the corruption of power. Jesus on the Cross
raises the standard of truth, seeking and living the truth, questioning the self-serving propaganda of the powerful in Church, in
State and in University. Only such devotion to the truth shall set
us free (John 8:32). Only such devotion to the truth enables us to
be justice-seekers and peace-makers to which disciples are called
in the Sermon on the Mount (Matt 5:6,9). The critical minds
which are prepared to take up the cross of truth-seeking and follow the example of Jesus are indeed his disciples.

It was a knowledge or truth above love for which Jesus was
martyred in Nietzsche's reflection. The love, the care and service
of God and of one another, which summarised the whole law and
prophets, was revealed in his ministry, in his care of the sick, the
hungry, the excluded. Truth was the way to freedom and justice and
peace in the fellowship of a renewed humanity. This Kingdom was

now possible, available, at hand and still to come. It was utterly divine gift and yet human responsibility, to be received and yet achieved. The graciousness of the God of Jesus could empower and incorporate authentic human activity in the development of a world inclusive and enriching of all. No longer the division of Jew or Gentile, bond or free, male or female, but all one in Christ (Gal 3:28f). Those who accept the vocation to truth, whose critical minds are trained to question the accepted answers and established powers, must follow through in service of the deprived or excluded. Otherwise the service of truth becomes self-service, place-seeking, adaptation to the powers which domesticate and inhibit truth. In University, in Church and notoriously in State, the best minds may be harnessed by a particular set of interests to produce a justifying ideology. The critical has turned uncritical and credulous in self-protection and self-promotion. The pursuit of truth has become too hazardous. The burden of that Cross may no longer be borne. The scene at Calvary must be deliberately blotted out.

Of course it cannot be. The Cross is discernible wherever the innocent suffer and the truth is crucified. Sorley MacLane captures all this for Scotland in his short poem, 'Calbharaigh':

> Chan eil mo shuil air Calbharaigh
> no air Bethlehem an aigh
> ach air cuil ghood an Glaschu
> far bheil an labhadh fais
> agus air seòmar an Dún-éideann
> seòmar bochdainn 's craidh
> far a bhail an naoidhean creuchdach
> ri aonagraich gu bhas.

> My eye is not on Calvary
> nor on Bethlehem the Blessed
> but on a foul-smelling backland in Glasgow,
> where life rots as it grows
> and on room in Edinburgh, a
> room of poverty and pain
> where the diseased infant
> writhes and wallows till death.

The critical mind which is not aware and questioning of

rotting human life and writhing infants, has lost its cutting edge and is no longer in alliance with the Cross.

And it may well be too much to ask of us, of our students, of anybody. Shall we not confine ourselves to the neat and rigorous exercises at which scholars can excel? Is this not our proper contribution to making and keeping the world human? So few are capable of being martyrs. Calvary is outside the city where the writ of civilised humanity runs. Let that be for the few saints or fanatics. Modest scholarship is for the many students and dons both possible and necessary and never to be despised.

So true. No real scholarship should ever be despised. But inherent in that learning process is the restless, questioning spirit. In all its activities there is a pain as well as a joy. Its most modest advances involve some painful disintegration of an older world with the joy that some new understanding is born. Dying to self in often very small ways is intrinsic to the life of learning, to the growth of truth. A personal world dies a little with every new development. This is painful and threatening to the self in its progress. Where the development extends beyond personal growth to the science itself, the pain and threat extend to the masters and students who must come to terms with a new truth. And the history of most disciplines reveals instances of masters and students resisting the new advance and its author as too threatening. Paradigmatic shifts in the sciences and humanities are only achieved at considerable pain for the protectors of the purity of the discipline and still more for the innovators. And still the questioning goes on so that power may not prevail at the expense of truth.

No discipline is an island. No scholar is removed from the needs of his neighbour. No university can cut itself off from the wider community and its problems, its untruths, injustices, lack of freedom and peace. The truly critical mind will raise his eye from the artificial confines of discipline and university and see outside the walls where for the critical and christian the question-mark of the Cross dominates the horizon. It is for the christian questioner to follow these questions and to carry his Cross as he pursues the knowledge for love. This is what finally marks us, in the old Irish phrase, as the servants of the King of the Friday.

If you can't Dance, you can't Pray

As I sought a theme for this Trinity Monday celebration, 'Holy Spirit' proved irresistible. There were texts in abundance but I preferred Paul's reflections on the gifts of the Spirit in 1 Corinthians 12, concentrating on verse 4: 'Now there are varieties of gifts but the same spirit'.

And then for a counter-theme, more earthy, rooted in and redolent of university, only 'human spirit' seemed appropriate and adequate. To complete this counter-point, a counter-text, celebratory, uniting the two moving spirits of christian rejoicing, and provoking perhaps a fresh youthful glance at the human face of God.

'If you can't dance, you can't pray' sounds at least irreverent and certainly excessive, particularly to someone unable to avail himself fully of the educational opportunities at the Ballrooms of Romance in the nineteen fifties. It does capture, however, something of the celebrating spirit which animates this day, this university, all good universities. Universities are above all temples of the spirit, the human spirit of course but a human spirit which in its diversity and creativity, community-making and celebration reaches for human perfection and beyond, for wholeness, even holiness. This morning, this day and this week we listen to the call of that human spirit as it expands us beyond the pinched and mean spirit of many a Monday morning, and sweeps us away in company with Kitty Stobling to follow the fiddler of Dooney and dance like the waves of the sea.

The Monday shadows are never easily evaded. The traditional Irish shadows still haunt us. Just beyond the gates, perhaps already within, lie our historic Irish enemies: poverty, unemployment, emigration and Irish-fighting-Irish. All now compounded by the creeping spectre of Aids and mushrooming nuclear clouds. Must the dance become a *danse macabre*? How much can the human spirit endure? How long can it survive?

As this university approaches its fourth centenary, as it

reflects on a much older and broader ranging of the human spirit, we may still take heart. For all the persistent destructiveness, the promethean distortions of humanity's soaring spirit, the creative capacities and achievements which this university symbolises allow us to go on hoping. That larger achievement of the human spirit in richer and fuller human community is still possible, partially achieved and worthy of celebration.

The hoping, enduring human spirit continues to search the scriptures of nature, of rock and seashore, of tissue and bone to read there in exquisite detail stories of mesons and quarks, of DNA, of species lost and species gained, of the advent and development of this very species, the species Reader. The species with the spirit of truth, with the ability to discover and check and share truth, to provide a home for it in university remains a crucial chapter in the scriptures of nature and yet transcends it. In its doubling-back on nature from which it emerged, the human spirit reads the scriptures that are given there while it creates new ones. In the modern university the discerning and creating are formally recognised and structured. Seasoned scholar and neophyte student join together in critical discernment of the given and in burgeoning creation of the new. Integrity and discipline in method and practice provide ascetical exercises for developing the human spirit en route to its perfection and wholeness. Where such integrity prevails and where wholeness is genuinely sensed and sought, the human spirit is no longer simply captive to the ambiguities and vanities to which all human flesh is heir. A holy-making process is at work.

The human spirit expresses and discerns the holy, the numinous, the awe-inspiring, the wonder of the world and the wonder of wondering at the world. It thus allows a further dimension to break through. Without the dramatic impact of Pentecost's mighty wind the spirit of the numinous, living God finds its own quiet expression in a hundred human activities, in a hundred university activities in library and laboratory. The work of discernment and creation reflects the Spirit who leads into all truth, whose brooding presence charts the way from chaos to creation. As it was in the beginning, is now and shall be at the end.

The university as temple to the human spirit yes, but as temple to the Holy Spirit? Even a university established in another age, one, as we may think, of faith, and dedicated to the Most Holy Trinity, could scarcely in these days of autonomous

secular disciplines and their towering achievements be readily
considered in terms of holiness and Holy Spirit. Yet the spirit of
created cosmos and of human creativity, the critical discerning
scholarly spirit, the spirit of communication and community-
making and community-serving, the spirit we invoke this very day,
the spirit of thanksgiving and celebration – human, true, but never
in a self-sufficient, self-enclosing way. The generous self-
transcending impulse of that spirit at its best reaches from and to
the mysterious and the numinous; in library and laboratory and not
just in chapel, we tread on holy ground. The dreams of the dream-
ing spires are of origins and destiny, of the miracle of the given
and of the hope for what is to come. We celebrate more than we
can ever know in the very halls where knowing is primary. Into all
truth in eschatological promise; that we may finally enter into the
ultimate mystery, truth at its source and climax. Openness to
that, reaching for that in wonder and integrity and humility, places
human spirit under the tuition of the Holy Spirit. It renders all
intellectual disciplines ways of sanctifying the human spirit;
making it holy too.

More modestly and hesitantly we confess with Cecil Day-
Lewis:

Spirit in whom we half believe
And would believe,
Free us from fear, revive us in
A fire of love.   *Requiem for the Living*

Modesty also dances. Hesitations and fears may humbly yield
to the fire of love as the Spirit called holy is also the spirit of joy
and celebration, of the good who are also merry, of the merry who
love to dance ('The Fiddler of Dooney'). The disciples who are
filled with joy and with the Holy Spirit (Acts 13:52) may be sure
this day of finding the living God 'satisfying (their) hearts with
food and gladness' (Acts 14:17). Dining-table and dance-floor
may join laboratory and library in manifesting and sharing the
fruits of the Spirit. Such 'are the varieties of gifts, but the same
Spirit (whose) manifestation is given for the common good' (1
Cor 12:4,7). The one Holy Spirit remains the basic guarantee of
the flourishing in community of the rich and diverse achievements
of human spirit which we celebrate this day.

In Liberating Memory

Homily at Memorial Mass for Kevin O'Higgins, Tim Coughlan, Archie Doyle, Bill Gannon

'Bear in mind these dead' was the simple and austere demand of the late John Hewitt. He dared 'not risk using that loaded word, Remember' and 'cannot urge or beg you/to pray for anyone or any-thing/for prayer in this green island/is tarnished with stale breath/worn smooth and characterless/as an old flagstone, trafficked/with journeys no longer credible/to lost generations.'

Daunted by 'the savage complications of our past', Hewitt confronted us with the dangers of Irish remembering. Our memorials like our monuments so easily weigh us down. We become the burden of our history. 'History may be servitude' (T.S. Eliot) but it may also be 'freedom'. 'This is the use of memory:/For liberation – not less of love but expanding/Of love beyond desire, and so liberation/From the future as well as the past.'

While we bear in mind these dead, Kevin O'Higgins, Tim Coughlan, Archie Doyle, Bill Gannon, we seek to do so in a liberating rather than enslaving spirit, the spirit which animates the readings from Ezechiel (36:22-28), Paul (1 Cor 11:23-26) and Matthew's acount of Jesus' Sermon on the Mount (Mt 5:38-48) which we have just heard.

The warnings of Ezechiel here and elsewhere are not far removed from those of Hewitt. Israel's profaning of Yahweh's name, a common cause of prophetic criticism, connects with the stale breath and incredible journeys to lost destinations of Irish prayer. In the verses immediately preceding his account of the Eucharist, Paul is sharply critical of the christian divisions which mar such celebrations. Jesus' summons to love of enemies could hardly be more strongly put. Warning and summons are also promise. A new heart, a heart of flesh to replace the heart of stone will come with God's own spirit which in Ezechiel's later vision will transform the valley of dry bones. The perfect love by which the

Father loves and to which christians are called by Jesus is promised and achieved for all in the forgiving and liberating death of Jesus. That is the liberating remembrance which, as Paul reminds his readers, is ours in the Eucharist. How far are we ready for that liberating memory. How far are we ready for Eucharist?

It can be so easy to march to Mass. In the Irish Catholic tradition it is the Mass that matters. Some of our best Masses, if one may use such language, are funeral Masses and memorial Masses. And yet we must always ask ourselves how far the memorial is, like the history, an expression of servitude or freedom? How far does it expand into love of enemies, or contract and leave us isolated with our own? If you love only those who love you and salute only your own brethren – in church as in market place!

We need to reflect again on what we do at Mass – on what we do in memory of Jesus, first of all, and then in memory of the four people whose names are put before us today, and beyond that, in memory of all our divided forebears. What we do at Mass, we do in symbol, in sign and sacrament, not in reduction of the reality but in enlargement of it. No christian can put a boundary to the march and reach of the Mass, the reach of two hands extended on a cross, to embrace all people and especially those for whose forgiveness he then prayed. In memory of Jesus is obviously in imitation of Jesus, following Jesus as disciples to the point of taking up one's cross, of forgiving one's enemies, of embracing the whole world. Of course the memory and remembering go further. We are called and enabled not just to imitate Jesus, to behave like him but to be him, to enter into his forgiving death and resurrection, to share his life and love. In memory of him is a dying with him so that we may share the fullness of life which he embodies, the divine life of love itself. Not just like him, but him. It is all way-out, fantastic, incredible, like John Hewitt's journeys. And yet we eat the body and drink the blood. We are what we eat and drink, Christ. Worthily, as Paul reminds us, in the very next verses of 1 Corinthians, and worthily by the earlier verses means not divided, not in factions, not the faction fighters for which we are so often criticised. And the first item on the agenda is a split; Brendan Behan on the Corinthians at Eucharist, on the Irish at Mass.

Do we dare do this in memory of Jesus and exclude strangers, opponents, enemies? And can we truly remember in Christ those who have gone divisively before us and fail to recognise their deeper present unity in Christ?

This divided island has much to repent and much to repair.
The heritage of our history has been so much servitude as Gael and
Gall; Irish, Scottish and English; Catholic and Protestant have
struggled to dominate and so enslave and so be enslaved. Our little
memorial today is a tiny symbol of deeper Irish divisions, of wider
human division from Belfast to Beirut to the Punjab, from Soweto
to San Salvador. Can the arms on the Cross stretch so far even for
us who have grown up with its reconciling reach and pride ourselves, God bless the mark, on our fidelity in the footsteps, the
agonising, broken footsteps of the Master on the via dolorosa, on
our fidelity to the Mass? The haunting question remains, if we cannot celebrate this Mass, can we celebrate any Mass? Amos had a
word about God's despising feasts and solemn assemblies and
burnt offerings because of injustice, neglect, exclusiveness (Amos
5). Jesus picks up the same theme in his criticism of the Pharisees
and in his injunction to his disciples to be reconciled before coming to make their offering (Mt 5:23f). For this we need expression, symbolic expression, for that is the deepest expression, the
expression of that which is deepest in us, our sharing in Christ, his
humanity and divinity, his death and resurrection.

Will you speak to Tim on Resurrection Day? What an
arrogant and absurd question! We might ask it more often, particularly at our memorial and above all at our Mass. Ireland seems
so crowded with people who proclaim oneness in Christ and look
forward to his coming again, and yet who have such difficulty in
greeting and accepting one another as Catholics or Christians or
simply Irish. By this will they be known as disciples! By this will
they be ready for Eucharist! The conventional obstacles to shared
Eucharist between christians of different denominations may
sometimes be less formidable than those between christians of
one. Eucharist as task as well as gift may be as challenging to a
group of Catholics as to a mixed group of Catholics and Protestants. This Mass and any Mass should challenge us as deeply as any
joint Eucharist between Catholics and Protestants.

In the slow journey to mutual acceptance in Ireland,
Eucharist should take its rightful place as a means as well as a
goal of unity. If we were to await complete unity and acceptance
among christians, even among Irish Catholics, Eucharist would
forever recede. Such a concept of Jesus' memorial would be a new
form of servitude. The gift, for which we are already unready, is
first of all gift and so carries its own readying and liberating force

today for ourselves and all the people of this island. It is, I believe, the final message of the four men we remember, now folded in the single party of God.

> We cannot revive old factions
> We cannot restore old policies
> Or follow an antique drum.
> These men, and those who opposed them
> and those whom they opposed
> Accept the constitution of silence
> And are folded in a single party.
>
> And all shall be well and
> All manner of thing shall be well
> By the purification of the motive
> In the ground of our beseeching.

T.S. Eliot

A Forgiven and a Forgiving People

Which is easier, to say to the paralytic, 'Your sins are forgiven' or to say, 'Rise, take up your pallet and walk'? (Mk 2:9)

As the miracles of modern medicine march on, the forgiveness which Jesus by the power of God released in the world, too frequently hesitates, stumbles and collapses. The forgiven and forgiving people which he established by his own power and example, from paralytic to executioners ('Father, forgive them', Luke 23:34), and by the commissioning of his disciples ('whose sins you shall forgive', John 20:23) has grown tired and unsure of itself. At least it retains the capacity to be surprised and refreshed by the sound of Jesus' forgiveness as it emerged from the rubble of Enniskillen in the voice of Gordon Wilson. Our gathering here today would make that forgiveness and forgiving our own. We would resume our commitment as a forgiven and forgiving people beyond the tragic destructiveness which still afflicts our island and our world. We would hope and pray that Enniskillen may not have been in vain; that those who died so innocently and those who survived so forgivingly would help finally to set us free from our mutual enslavement and destruction.

In this 'Advent-darkened room' (Patrick Kavanagh), hope is focused on the birth of 'a child born to capsize (our) values and wreck (our) equipoise' (Louis MacNeice). From Enniskillen to Bethlehem disciples of Christ walk a stony, painful road in search of a place hospitable to the child, in search of a people receptive, in search of a self which in St Paul's words will allow the vulnerable, loving, forgiving Christ to shape its life. That birth of Christ in each disciple has been so often deferred, cancelled, fought against, fled from. Christmas 1987 is yet another summons to let the Christ struggling to be born in each christian life emerge. For Irish disciples the summons has become more urgent. Eliot's Magi wondered:

> ... were we led all that way for
> Birth or Death? There was a Birth certainly
> We had evidence and no doubt. I had seen birth and death
> But had thought they were different; this Birth was
> Hard and bitter agony for us, like Death, our death.

Irish disciples confess: 'There was Death certainly'. And Birth? Will the 'hard and bitter agony' of Enniskillen be no more than death's despairing struggle or will it prove to be the birth-pangs of new, divine Christlife born in us and to us? Are we sharing the road to Bethlehem or remaining alien, unforgiving peoples clutching our alien gods?

The child of the new covenant, the child who is the new covenant which is to be written in our hearts, is to break the cycle of alienation. 'Knocking the heads of Church and State together' in MacNeice's image, this Christ-child opens the way for new beginnings when the mighty may no longer cling to their thrones and the despised and rejected go first into the kingdom. Beginning from a manger in a stable, the ultimate source and power of love in the world went forth to convert the world by love and forgiveness, to establish that kingdom where righteousness and peace would kiss (Ps 85), where 'all shall know me from the least to the greatest, says the Lord; for I will forgive their iniquity, and I will remember their sin no more' (Jer 31:34).

The birth of Christ, as divine forgiveness made human to forgive and transform humanity, is the christian counterpoint to the murderous destruction of Enniskillen and its parallels. At this Advent time it suggests our responsibility to release that loving forgiveness in our island. The forgiving God of Israel and of Jesus in continuous search of a repentant people must be released anew in Ireland. Only our authentic transformation into a forgiven and forgiving people will match the reach of divine ambition and of our desperate human need. For that to be achieved we need symbols, signs and actions, practices.

An annual Forgiveness Sunday celebrated as an inter-church event in the Advent Season would help liberate us forgivingly to one another. Without prayer and its communal, ecumenical expression, we will not be opened up to the subversive power of the child of Bethlehem.

Human prayer and the symbols of the divine love and forgiveness must become 'heaven in ordinarie' daily life and organisation. It is not, I believe, too harsh to say that the ecumenical movement for all its efforts lacks the popular involvement and dynamic activity usually associated with a social change. While the politicians search for political solutions, as they must, perhaps a dynamic and popular ecumenical movement could provide the context of divine love and forgiveness in which the right political moves are more quickly discerned and more easily made. If Enniskillen is not to fade with all its counterparts to become another forgotten atrocity, christians must take initatives as christians. A network of christian groupings meeting regularly north and south, travelling regularly north and south, getting to know, to understand, to forgive and to create, could provide the beginnings of a forgiven and forgiving people. That we may know that the son of man has power on earth to forgive sin, we must at his word get up and walk.

The Girl Next Village

This is a resurrection occasion. Not only in the sense that every truly christian occasion is a resurrection occasion because it takes place, Easter Sunday fashion, in the after-glow and by the power of Jesus Christ risen from the dead. It is that also in the sense that, by the assumption, our risen Lord, with infinite filial sensitivity, extended in a special way to his Mother and ours a share in his resurrection. That gift of filial love we celebrate today by laying the foundation of a new church, a new shelter for God and his people, which will bear the name of that Mother as she is particularly and traditionally honoured by Irish Catholics.

A new church is a new beginning; a beginning based, as St Paul insists, on no other foundation than the risen Lord himself. The fruits of the resurrection will be shared here in word and sacrament by generations born anew by being baptised into the death and resurrection of the Lord. For a church is a people before it is a building; a risen people, people who already share the risen life of Jesus but still await its fulfilment. But if a new church is a beginning, it is also, in the richly paradoxical way of humanity and christianity, a completion. The church, people and building, the emergence of which we honour today, marks the end of almost a hundred years of pilgrim faith and prayer, which has brought to this obscure bogside village in Mayo, thousands and hundreds of thousands of believing and praying people from all over Ireland and in these latter years from all over the globe. It must seem a rather unimposing centre to have attracted so many and such diverse people, to have proved the focal point of such intense faith and prayer. If I might presume on being a neighbour's child, just a few miles down the bog road, I might readily concede that Knock, by nature or creation, hardly gave promise of being such a meeting-point for the world on the Feast of the Assumption 1874.

That christian paradox has been at work again. Didn't somebody make an even more trenchant comment in the gospel on a village which 2,000 years ago can hardly have been any more imposing than Knock was a century ago? 'Can anything good come out of Nazareth?' And yet in that miserable little Near Eastern village the incredible occurred: the final breakthrough in human history began. In that obscure village an obscure woman of faith and prayer acceded to the gracious request of the Almighty God to become the Mother of his Son. By courtesy of Mary, God broke through to man in Jesus Christ and man broke through to God. By courtesy of Mary we also are called and are sons of the Father.

One hundred years ago the living faith of equally obscure Knock villagers, again by courtesy of Mary, picked up the signals of that divine breakthrough in a manner which has proved an inspiration and reassurance to succeeding generations. Knock has now become a minor Nazareth, where men may bow with Mary's faith and hope and love in a never-ending 'Be it done unto me according to your word, Lord.'

One cannot simply judge a place by its landscape or townscape, but by its people. But the people of nineteenth-century Knock were ordinary – as ordinary as the people of first-century Nazareth or the pilgrims from twentieth-century Belfast or Boston or Birmingham. A further aspect of christian paradox – the ordinary as witness of the extraordinary, the mighty put down from their throne, as Mary proclaimed it, and the humble exalted, the wisdom of this world confounded by the foolishness of God. As if to emphasise how truly divine the divine is, when it takes human form, it seeks out the most ordinary, unimposing human form in case human power or prestige or wealth should somehow distract from the radically different divine. If grace, as St Thomas puts it, perfects or completes human nature, it also appears to delight at times in mocking it – at least the pretentious manifestations of it. The church which we commence today at Knock is a monument to all that is ordinary and therefore best in the human as it is taken up in grace and faith to recognise that 'he who is mighty has done great things (to it) and holy is his name' (Luke 1:49).

Healing

The pilgrim faith and prayer of Knock have had the original evangelical quality of healing: the faith that makes whole by the power of Jesus, healing the sick of our own era. In so many ways Knock expresses the gospel care of Jesus for the sick on whom he expended so much of his time and energy with all the delicacy of a caring mother as he had experienced it in those formative years in

Nazareth. That the new church will be above all designed to cater in the most effective way for the sick, underlines Knock's traditional christian priorities.

The bodily healing was always for Jesus a sign of a deeper personal healing and reconciliation, and here the faith and prayer of Knock have remained deeply faithful to their Master.'Your sins are forgiven you' was at once more wonderful and more challenging than 'Take up your bed and walk'. The daily miracles of healing and reconciliation in the confessional, at personal prayer and at Mass have been experienced by countless pilgrims to Knock, alert to Mary's instructions to the wine-waiters at Cana: 'Do whatever he shall say to you' (John 2:5).

The healing and reconciling work of Mary's Son recognises the close link between the personal and the social. In our divided world the divisions of Jew and Gentile, bond and free, male and female continue to plague us long after they have been overcome in principle by Jesus' saving achievement. In our own island the divisions have taken a newly murderous turn. The people who assemble at this national shrine recognise the potential for hate, murder's spiritual father, which affects all of us and must surrender to the reconciling love for which Mary too suffered as she watched her Son offer himself on Calvary so that the spirit of hate and murder might be finally exorcised.

Nowhere is this division more distressing than between the christian Churches themselves. A further distressing aspect of this scandalous division is the way Mary, mother of the reconciler, of the Christ of unity, can be invoked to foster rather than overcome division. It is most important that we Catholics who cherish Mary so highly together with our Eastern Orthodox brothers and sisters, and indeed many Anglicans and other christians, should not allow the wonderful tradition to suffer from any doctrinal distortion or self-indulgent sentimentality, so unworthy of Mary. She always remained in the shadow of the central figure of Jesus and did so at Calvary in a way that is judgment on all sentimentalism. It is no less important that our fellow-christians who did not share this tradition of devotion to Mary should endeavour to understand and respect ours as it really is and not as it may be falsely purveyed by friend or critic. Mutual understanding between christians of different traditions, particularly in Ireland with its richly Catholic Marian piety, demands in Christ's own name, a serious attempt by all the Churches to exercise a loving fairness and respect in this

sensitive area of the role of Mary. It is for tasks like this that
Mary is traditionally honoured as type and model of the Church. In
her faith and hope and trust, she could provide inspiration for the
work of reflection, exploration and interpretation by which the
Church strives to deepen its understanding, purify its faith and
present the ancient gospel ever anew to succeeding generations
and in face of different problems and crises. The questioning of
the angel in the annunciation story: 'How can these things be?'
(Luke 1:34); the glorious interpretation of God's saving work in
her proclaimed on the occasion of her visit to Elizabeth (the
Magnificat, Luke 1:39); the way she reflected on the manifestations at Bethlehem 'when she kept all these things, pondering
them in her heart' (Luke 2:19); a reaction recorded again after
Jesus had been lost and found in the Temple (Luke 2:5) – all these
offer an outline of the Church's questioning, reflection and
proclamation in the task we call theology.

The classical description of theology is 'faith seeking
understanding'. Mary, in common with every true christian since,
sought for such understanding. But our faith is a prayer-faith. As
recognition of God and his saving love in Jesus Christ, immediately our faith launches into the praise of 'Hallowed be thy name'
and 'My soul doth magnify the Lord' or the petition of 'Give us
this day our daily bread and forgive us our trespasses.' And this
faith is most fully realised and expressed in the Eucharist. So
close and unbreakable is the relation, that the Church seeking to
undersand its faith in theology might well be rewritten as the
Church trying to think through the meaning of its prayer.

A prayerless theology then is no theology at all. It is not
possible for a member of the Church to contribute to its interpretation, articulation and presentation of its own deeper life, its
prayer life to the Father and the Son by the gift of the Spirit, without entering more and more into that prayer-life. Of course every
prayerful member of the Church is a thoughtful member who
makes his own contribution to the explicit self-understanding of
the Church. Yet there are people with more specialised training,
opportunity and responsibility, who under the authority of the
Church's official teachers, the Pope and the bishops, seek to
explore more systematically that developing life of the Church as
it makes its pilgrim way to the Father. Part of their task is to
explore also, after the reflective fashion of Mary herself, Mary's
role in this pilgrimage of salvation in which all men are engaged

and in the prayer life which provides its sustenance and meaning on
the way. It is part of the burden of human weakness that they may in
common with other christians perform their task inadequately or
unhelpfully at times and that even when they are at their most adequate and helpful they may be misunderstood or misrepresented.

Part of Knock's reconciling message must be to overcome
any apparent division between the theologian and the devout. Cut
off from prayer there can be no genuine theology. The truly devout
are never unthinking or narrow whether they are characterised by
the restless voyaging of a Francis Xavier or the healing concern of
a Father Damien, the global vision of a house-bound Thérèse of
Lisieux or the universal sympathy with such diverse men and movements which was shown by that pious farmer's son from Bergamo we
call Pope John.

Prayerless theology is the intellectual version of the whited
sepulchre with its beautifully-polished exterior but within full of
dead men's bones and all uncleanness (Mt 23:27). Thoughtless
devotion 'may', in Jesus' words, 'heap up empty phrases as the
Gentiles do: for they think that they will be heard for their many
words' (Mt 6:7) or it may turn to the public relations of those who
say 'Lord, Lord, but do not the will of the Father who is in heaven.'
Prayer and theology belong together. Apart they powerfully illus-
trate, again in Jesus' words 'the house which divided against itself
must fall'. May the new beginning which this occasion represents
enable the prayerful and the thoughtful woman of Nazareth to
play her part in uniting the heart and mind of the Church in a
loving and fruitful way.

Theology represents only one specialised aspect of the
Church's thoughtfulness based on its faith and prayer. The concern
we see manifest here in care of the sick, the service of
reconciliation throughout Ireland and the world, is that active
manifestation of the thoughtfulness which is demanded of all
those who call Jesus Lord. And there is still so much to be done for
the neglected and marginal peoples of the world, for whole
countries, even continents of them; nearer home whole classes of
them like the prisoners or parentless children or deserted wives or
one-parent families, or, more recognised if no less neglected,
people like the aged or the lonely. The living prayer of Knock pilgrims must surely seek expression in attending to these personally
in so far as possible and endeavouring to correct the society which
has ignored or exploited them.

Prayer and reflection, healing and caring are all aspects of that one christian response of love of God and of our neighbour which Jesus embodied and Mary so faithfully exemplified. From prayer to reflection and service and so deeper into prayer must be the message of Knock in the future as it was in the past.

As I said, this is a resurrrection occasion. A new church that will be a new symbol of the life-giving presence of the risen Christ, is erected in response to the prayerful faith of generations of Irish people. This faith has always aligned itself with the faith of her who responded so fully and deeply from Nazareth to Calvary and beyond. In preparation for the building of the first church, the establishment of God's people or the *ecclesia*, which preceded any public building, she devoted herself to prayer with the apostles in the room in Jerusalem as they awaited the Spirit which was poured forth at Pentecost (Acts 1:14). We join today in that resurrection and pentecostal expectancy. We look forward with her to future generations of pilgrims who will enjoy shelter from the winds and rains of Mayo as they open their hearts Mary-wise to the healing and reconciling power of that Spirit, which was gained for us at such cost by her Son.

A Marriage Homily

So faith, hope, love abide, these three; but the greatest of these is love (1 Cor 13:13).

That there should be such love that through the detours of the last two years has led James and Siobhan here: that we celebrate. For that we give thanks. Not that we think of it as simply exciting and for the young easy, the natural fruit of an inevitable relationship.

The story of their love, as of any love, is exciting, but it couldn't have been easy for them as it has never been for us. All the more reason to rejoice today as their love finds decisive expression in this public commitment called marriage. Public commitment that goes beyond this particular public, their families and friends to the wider public who will gradually come to know Mr and Mrs O'Hanlon. Today's commitment in love goes further and deeper as in this, its sacramental expression, it calls not just ourselves or a wider public but God's self to witness it. What James and Siobhan bestow on each other today, their own selves, they do by the power and in the presence of ultimate love. As God should be their witness. Almost too serious for words, even words as sacred as 'I love' or 'I take you to be my husband'.

Serious and sacred but not too solemn. Party-goer Jesus made sure in the evangelist John's story of Cana that there was plenty of good wine. Indeed by that account he gave the first public witness to his vocation and power as Son of God at the wedding reception. The burden of Jesus' vocation never kept him from eating and drinking with his friends while John the Baptist and his disciples were more given to fasting. Vocation by the same father of Jesus Christ, who today calls Siobhan and James together into a new community of life and love, is also a matter for celebration. Whatever the difficulties of the road just tread or of the one ahead, the love that has brought them before us and before God is rooted in their own personal richness, in support and care by us, their families and friends and in that inexhaustible source of loving we call God.

It is a powerful but obscure word, love. We can become obsessed by the sound of it and dazzled by the mystery of it. It can bewitch, excite or depress us by its promise for the future or frustration from the past. What we need to remember above all is that it is an active word, a transitive verb. I love you. You love me. That action and that transitiveness have effects. As love acts, it effects. It produces results in the lover and in the beloved. The results vary in quality and in kind. Nobody could classify and assess them all. Some kinds of effects and results are particularly relevant today.

Love is creative. The spark of love which brought these strangers together, the parents of James and of Siobhan, all our parents, issued in the life we know, in the beings we are. That kind of creation, procreation, is a crucial effect of human loving. Parents' love for their infant strangers is creative of the children and their own future identity. We become who we are by loving and being loved. Indeed we do so first by being loved in our infant incapacity.

The creative interaction between James and Siobhan, which has brought them here today, has identified and defined them in a new way. They are not the people they were before they met and loved. Being-in-love, loving and being loved with that intensity develops new dimensions. 'I never saw him do that before' says mother wistfully. 'You would never believe the change in her.' And the creativity will, must go on for them and for us. Their new love can rekindle our own and release creative powers grown tired or stunted. We too share in the overspill of fresh love and new commitent.

It may seem premature to refer to a second power of love, its healing power. Yet Siobhan and James have undoubtedly experienced it in the arms of their parents during their childhood years. The hurts that go deeper and come later are more a part of the rest of us. We all need to be reminded of this healing power of love. Today that healing power spreads from James and Siobhan into their future which cannot be simply untroubled but whose troubles will certainly yield, perhaps in unexpected ways, to healing by love. Their healing love spreads out to us also, their co-celebrators and concelebrants of this marriage. For me and I hope for all of us, a new pledge of love in marriage reaches in healing fashion to hurts that still linger, to losses, pains and failures never quite removed.

'It's a new life, James', friends say jocosely yet seriously. Yeats' 'A Terrible Beauty is Born' sounds rather sinister, but so much is 'changed, changed utterly'. That transforming quality of love which takes clear shape in the choice and commitment of marriage restructures all a couple's relationships. As they marry, they reset the world. A new heaven and a new earth provide the context for their new life together.

The transformation in unity or into unity takes time to adjust to. It has its own strains and stresses. It will require respect and patience and tolerance, the slow growth of affection and friendship, as well as the buzz and excitement of being-in-love and making love. It can sound drab enough today but the growth of husband and wife into friendship is an extraordinary achievement. And that too, we their friends would wish for Siobhan and James. That too will give this day an even greater significance as they recall it for children and grandchildren, friends and neighbours.

A story of human loving with creative, healing and transforming powers is what we witness today, what we celebrate with the ministers of their sacrament, James and Siobhan. The word 'sacrament' reveals the deeper point of the story.

Creating, healing and transforming is the story of God's love of Israel and humanity as prophets such as Hosea and Isaiah realised. It is the story of Jesus as we follow it through the Gospels. Sent out of love, he lived and died by love as the new Lord of Creation in stilling storms and changing water into wine, feeding the hungry and raising the dead. And so much of his time was healing time for the physically, mentally and spiritually ill. As he laid down his life for his friends, he inaugurated in resurrection the new life of the Spirit of God in which we all share through faith and baptism. A new heaven and a new earth, a new creation was among us and available to us. All had been changed utterly. Creative, healing and transforming love had taken flesh in Jesus and had taken root in our world ineradicably.

Early disciples of Jesus, in the first centuries after his death and resurrection, saw the connection between the story of God's love of Israel, the story of Jesus and the loving union of husband and wife. The Pauline letter to the Ephesians had already elaborated on it. And so the christian community divined the divine, God-involved significance of christian marriage. They recognised it as a sacrament, a symbolic realisation of the power and presence of the God who is love.

What we witness today, what we celebrate and participate in, the loving commitment of James and Siobhan as husband and wife, opens them and us up to the ultimate mystery of life, the love which is God.

Preaching and Conversion

The Liturgy of the Word – at Mass, in the other sacraments and as constituting a service of worship on its own – may be one of the more successful elements in our liturgical renewal. Not all the readings, particularly on weekdays from the Old Testament, are capable of inspiring or even connecting with a particular congregation. Yet the regular, organised reading of the Bible and the employment of a range of readers from the community should encourage much greater involvement and familiarity with the Word of God as written and spoken.

Critical to the effectiveness of the Liturgy of the Word is the homily or sermon. The method and manner of such preaching, its success and failure, the diverse approaches and resources available, have been the subject of much discussion. Here I want to reflect on one aspect of the preacher's role which may be easily overlooked and which, despite its limited perspective, sheds some light on the relationship between Word of God and sermon, preacher and community, relationships which enter into the preparation, presentation and consequences (if any!) of the sermon.

The model of all our preaching derives from Jesus, his predecessors in John the Baptist and the prophets, and his immediate successors in the apostles and first disciples. The proclamation of God's Word by Jesus (the kerygma) was the proclamation of the decisive time (the kairos) of the kingdom or kingly rule of God. In the apostolic preaching this becomes the proclamation of Jesus as risen, as Christ, as Lord, as the actual and definitive inauguration of the history of God's final, saving and loving rule and power. The announcing of this divine gift embodied the divine summons to respond to it, to accept it in faith, to be converted and live out the new life in Christ, the kingdom life. The summons to conversion implied a judgment on previous life in darkness and sin and held the promise of new and transformed life to be expressed in love of God and love of neighbour.

The 'conversion' dimension of preaching, as illustrated in

and even constitutive of the New Testament, does not exactly strike one in speaking or listening to the modern sermon. There is sometimes a considerable amount of moral exhortation, general or specific, but that does not reveal the deeper conversion to which people are summoned in the New Testament. Metanoia or conversion is the turning in faith and trust to the loving Father but it is a movement from darkness to light, from blindness to vision, from sickness to health, from sheer lack of awareness to profound and transforming recognition of the God and Father of Jesus Christ. It is much more then than the limited moralistic change to which it is sometimes reduced. It is a continuing rediscovery of the God and Father of Jesus. A rediscovery is continually necessary because of our continually obscuring of the true face of God by our human idols. It is continually possible because the Word of God which the preacher proclaims is not only the Word of judgement, capable of revealing to us our condition and unmasking our idols, but the same dynamic movement of the Word carries the power to transform, enlighten and liberate us from the old slavery.

Attending to the conversion structure of the Liturgy of the Word undoubtedly discloses a real and possibly neglected dimension. It does not immediately and clearly distinguish it from much of the other sacramental, pastoral and teaching work of the Church. All of this has an underlying conversion structure, based on God's initiating gift and the community's personal call and response or refusal. Some further specification is necessary.

The ecclesia (*qahal*) is the assembly of the called, summoned by the Word of God and accepting that Word in faith and conversion. The entry into the christian community by faith and baptism, the self-realisation of the community as christian in the Eucharist, the sacramental revealing of the unity of Christ and his Church as matrimony, all involve and require the word of power. In the post-Reformation tradition, however, we have only recently rediscovered the Liturgy of the Word itself and that the assembly it convokes is also a profound and typical realisation of the Church, local and universal. That the Church is realised in this way in the Eucharistic celebration we have always recognised, but we see more clearly now that this also happens in services of the Word, something the tradition of reciting and singing in community the daily hours only intermittently conveyed. If the Church is discovering, realising and transforming itself in the light and by the power of the Word, the Word's special liturgy may not be seen

merely as a kind of pedagogical preparation for the real action at
the Mass or as a fashionable substitute for devotions such as Bene-
diction or the Monday night Novena that no longer appeal to
certain parishioners.

Acceptance of the Liturgy of the Word as a central and
necessary expression of the Church's identity and activity will
help correct magical tendencies in approaching the sacraments.
It will make the Bible essential reading and study for all Catholics that they may be effectively nourished by the Word of God. It
will place greater responsibility on the priest as community
leader to insure he is familiar with and constantly fed by the Word.
In terms of ecumenical celebrations such acceptances of the Liturgy of the Word as realising the saving and reconciling presence
of God in Jesus Christ, as constituting the assembly of his people,
would express and promote the unity already existing, in an
authentic and liberating way. It should not, however, be simply
adopted and devised as a technique for praying together to escape
the difficulties of joint Eucharist. That would be to devalue it.
The particular significance of inter-Church liturgies of the Word
is related to its conversion structure, as christians and communities from different traditions turn to their one God and to one another.

The community of the Word is formed by the single dynamic
process of proclamation and conversion. The proclamation
through reading and preaching contains in itself the power to
judge, to open the eyes of the blind, to elicit the faith response of
conversion and embody that in new life. But all this is directed to
the foundation and formation of the new life of a community. It is
as a community that christians turn to God in Jesus Christ, his ultimate Word. Conversion to God is also conversion to the community. The deepest thrust of the summons and power of the Word
is to conversion of the community to its God and to itself. To
parphrase St John, if one is not converted to his neighbour whom
he sees, how can one be converted to God whom he does not see?
Continuing formation of christian community by constant conversion to the neighbour and so to God, constitutes the essential task
of preaching.

The preacher is a member of that christian community. He
also stands under the judgment of the Word. He too is in need of
conversion. His conversion is part of the community's conversion,
for as a christian he can be converted only in and through the

community. The preacher, as announcer and proclaimer of conversion to the community, must further see himself as involved in the community's process of conversion. Even as he mediates and announces the faith of the tradition to which the community is to respond, he is articulating the faith of the community. He is not only speaking to, but also out of the community. His leadership is a leadership of the community as a member of it.

As he stands together with the community under the judgment, summons and transforming power of the Word, he will give the lead in conversion. Otherwise, he fails as leader. The power of the Word of God is not finally tied to any particular human instrument. Yet the preacher's failure to respond in faith, to give the lead in conversion, creates a discord and disruption in the community. It involves his own condemnation for failing to discern the Word of the Lord.

The sermon should be the initiation of the community's conversion process by expressing the beginnings of the preacher's own conversion to deeper awareness and fuller acceptance of the Lord and of the neighbour, of the community. It is not, therefore, merely an explanatory doctrinal word or a moral exhortation to others, although both these may be involved. It is a fresh articulation of personal and communal faith which opens the preacher and the community to the mysteries of incarnation, death and resurrection of Jesus Christ, of God achieving fulfillment in man. Such faith has to be constantly restored and renewed in a hundred different contexts and with a thousand different implications and applications.

The preacher as convert, and the sermon as conversion of the preacher, provide a unity and coherence to the Liturgy of the Word similar to that of the Eucharist, where the priest and the people enter into the saving act of Jesus Christ. The people in the Liturgy of the Word are no more passive listeners than they are passive spectators at the Eucharist. The preacher is no more isolated from and simply set over and against his audience than the chief celebrant of the Eucharist. Liturgy, by definition, is an action, and an action of the people. In the Liturgy of the Word the faith to be proclaimed and the conversion to be achieved are common to preacher and congregation.

At a different level the speech-act, as it is sometimes called, enters into the definition, formation and development of the self. The old cocktail party chestnut: 'How do I know what I think of President Carter's mission to the Middle East until I say it?' has its point. We do discover what we think in speaking. We even discover what we are. In authentic and committed speech, we determine what we become. Our lives are shaped by our actions, but some of the most important of these actions are speech-actions. In an authentic life where the shaping is consistent, there will be continuity between speech-actions and other actions. So it will be fair to say that a man is what he says. And such speech action which is life-shaping occurs all the time. It is a process intermingled with the process of the rest of our lives. So through word and deed we gradually form the dominant pattern of our lives.

The application of all this to the preacher is fairly obvious. His sermon as speech-act is an experience of his authentic faith, seeking anew God and the neighbour. In the context of listening to the Word of God and articulating a faith response to it, he speaks under judgement on the blindness and failure of himself and his community. His sermons will reflect awareness of this judgement but still more the summons and the power to turn again. In his words the turning again in faith will find expression, revealing his own fresh shaping of his life, his conversion process. By sharing this shaping and conversion he hopes to stimulate and articulate the conversion in faith of his congregation. The preacher whose words do not express his conversion, has nothing to share with his congregation. His moral right to articulate their faith and lead their conversion is undermined.

Such a view of preaching may be more frightening in some respects. Yet it clears the way for the preacher's surrender to the Word of God in faith and conversion as the primary requirement. It unites preacher and congregation in a common enterprise. And it indicates the intrinsic connection between the Word as heard and preached in the Liturgy and the Word as enacted in the rest of life.

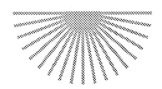

PART FIVE

Meditation: *Faith at the Fringe*

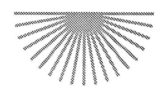

Creative Christians

All of us, in our faith, as in our humanity, feel we exist much of the time at the fringe in relation to God as well as in relation to one another and to the cities and states in which we live. Not many of us occupy the seats of the powerful. Even the powerful often find themselves sent to the fringe by their very power which can be para ysing; unable as they are to move themselves or to move others.

Into that kind of world there came a man who was once introduced by Philip to Nathaniel as likely Messiah from Nazareth. Obvious retort: 'Can anything good come out of Nazareth?' (Jn 1:46). One is speaking of a fringe province in a great empire far from the centres of power. Within that fringe province, a fringe village called Nazareth. And his own people said of him later, when he preached and worked his miracles there, 'Is this not the carpenter, son of Joseph and Mary?' And even his family, disturbed by his activity, came to find him, to take him away because, as they said, 'He is beside himself.' That's the kind of fringe person I hope to put before you in these four meditations.

For today I want to talk about the astonishing creativity of this fringe person and the creativity that he releases in all at the fringe, and about the creative people who often have to exist at the fringe because the structures of any organisation can take only so much creativity. The most creative, the exceptional, the people we call artists, were described by a great twentieth-century theologian, Paul Tillich, as the 'latent Church'. But we are all artists. We all have our creative gift. We all have to live, to create a life that nobody else can reproduce. There is one 'original' we must all do. That's the original of our own lives.

Let us think for a moment of this creativity. Coming from the childhood fringe, as it were, we enter a circle, a society. Our way of contact, claiming, defining our place is to make a sentence. The creativity that came in Jesus is described as the 'Word of God made flesh'. The word of the human spirit, as it is made flesh even in the simplest sentence, is part of that creativity. Jesus was a lover of words, a maker of sentences, a creator of parables, a teller of stories. But all that was to express the parable of God's love alive in the world. What we need to remember, as we live at the fringe, is our artistic vocation to shape the word of God in our own flesh. As we do that, we will often find ourselves at odds with one another, out of tune with the world. We will find ourselves, as Jesus did, thought perhaps by our families to be 'beside ourselves'. We may find ourselves even pushed further to the fringe and beyond the fringe on to a cross on Calvary. To appreciate the flesh which the Word of God became, we must understand that kind of strangeness, and how we ourselves may be estranged. But we must understand it in the context of a world created by God in which we were given the creative gift. We may look foolish, we may not sound sensible, but we could be the clown-creators who are, also in that vision, often the rejected.

There is a marvellous picture of this in a poem by the American poet, e.e. cummings:

> a bespangled clown
> standing on eighth street
> handed me a flower.
> Nobody, it's safe
> to say, observed him but
> myself; and why? because
> without any doubt he was
> whatever (first and last)
> mostpeople fear most:
> a mystery for which i've
> no word except alive
> that is, completely alert
> and miraculously whole;
> with not merely a mind and a heart
> but unquestionably a soul –
> by no means funereally hilarious
> (or otherwise democratic)
> but essentially poetic
> or ethereally serious:
> a fine not a coarse clown
> (no mob, but a person)
> and while never saying a word
> who was anything but dumb;

> since the silence of him
> self sang like a bird.
> Mostpeople have been heard
> screaming for international
> measures that render hell rational
> – i thank heaven somebody's crazy
> enough to give me a daisy

It's back to the daisies, to the lilies of the field, to our ability to see the creation of God about us, to feel the creating of God within us. That's what was opened up by this man from the fringe we call Jesus Christ.

It's hard to attend to what's happening within us even as we move and speak, as we look at the world about us, to attend to that creating and creative element. Without us and our creativity, the poet would speak in vain. He needs his creative listeners and readers, as the painter needs his creative viewers, as the stage needs its creative audiences. And it's in that exchange between poet and reader, between stage and audience, picture and viewer, that the spark occurs again, the spark that occurred when God created the world out of nothing; the creation that came from chaos. As we put our sentences together we are overcoming the chaos. It takes fringe people to remind us of the real humanity of that man Jesus and of those people, ourselves. It's in the listening to the music that we may be moved, as the heroine, for example, of Carson McCuller's book The Heart is a Lonely Hunter was moved as she listened to Beethoven's Third Symphony. 'But maybe the last part of the symphony was the music she loved best, glad and like the greatest people in the world, running and springing up in a hard, free way. Wonderful music like this was the worst hurt there could be. The whole world was this symphony and there was not enough of her to listen.'

The movement from wonder, excitement, pleasure, enrichment, to pain and frustration, is charted there. There is not enough of us to listen even to one symphony. There is certainly not enough of us to take in the symphony of the world. But there is so much of us, and there is so much that is dormant and undeveloped, and there is so much that Jesus releases for us but not without the pain. Our growth, our development, our creation is also our pain. In pain we are born, and in pain we die, but above all in pain we live, live into the next phase, into the next development. The mystery of the pain associated with creation which we hear so effectively from the creative people we call artists, we know in ourselves. Every mother and father has known the pain of creation. The poem or painting or child, the self-creation in which God engages us, in which we are his co-partners, is born of the pain, and that pain reflects isolation, rejection and a dying to oneself. Our very existence can be shattered, our hearts broken, our minds bruised as we move, move through the pains of growth into some new creation.

Celebration is part of the artist's gift to us and it was such a part of Jesus' own life (a scandalous part; he was a great party-man and the parties were always with the wrong crowd – the sinners and the harlots and the publicans). All that celebration in his life, beginning his public life in John's gospel with a wedding party and ending in all the gospels with a farewell party – all that part of him that celebrated the world, is part of us needing to celebrate. But all that part of him had also to live with the shadow side, had to live and to die by the isolation and rejection and execution that was his.

We sometimes sharply distinguish in our thinking, between, as we say, creation and redemption; between God's first loving, creative, throwaway act and then God's further attempt to rescue us. Perhaps on further reflection there is an inner unity and continuity. Perhaps we too sharply differentiate between creation and redemption or, as Paul calls it 'new creation'. Pain may be the necessary way forward. The artist in the pain of his creation, or the frustration he may suffer, can again help us to understand this continuity in our own lives, in our history and beyond our history.

The clergyman poet, R.S. Thomas, recounts his presence on the stage as Fritz Kreisler was playing. There was no room, so he was pushed into a seat along the side of the stage. He could watch Kreisler closely as he goes on:

I could see, to, the twitching of the fingers,
Caught temporarily in art's neurosis,
As we sat there or warmly applauded
This player who so beautifully suffered
For each of us upon his instrument.
So it must have been on Calvary
In the fiercer light of the thorn's halo:
The men standing by and that one figure,
The hands bleeding, mind bruised but calm,
Making such music as lives still.

And no one daring to interrupt
Because it was himself that he played
And closer than all of them the God listened.

Without the listeners there would be no art, without the listening God, no redemption. In our listening as in our speaking, in our movements to and from one another, there is the pain and the resurrection, the dying and rising again. The fringe figure opens out to us the continuity between these three gardens: the Garden of Eden – one foot in Eden as we like to think of ourselves; the Garden of Gethsemane – 'if it be possible let this pass from me'; and the garden where Mary met the man she thought was the gardener and found it was the Lord – risen.

The continuity between all that creativity resumed in the life of Jesus Christ, expressed in the life of all of us, summarises the relationship between cosmos and God. We think of ourselves still, perhaps as at the centre of the cosmos. Science has opened up to us vast vistas which show how planet Earth is as peripheral as my home village of Bekan or Jesus' village of Nazareth. But the peripheral is always at the same distance from God as any other part of the cosmos, and has the same closeness, and those of us who listen can pick up something of the closeness as well as being puzzled by the distance. The Jesus who prayed 'Let this chalice pass from me' was struggling between the distance and the closeness. Surely the Father would respond to the beloved Son. But the distance prevailed as he cried out 'My God, My God, why have you foresaken me?' And the distance was another boundary he had to go through before Mary could say 'Rabboni, Master' in the garden.

Such is the shape of our lives. We live at the distance and yet, as St Augustine said, 'with the God who is closer to me than my own soul'.

This fringe existence we live through, with the God occasionally breaking through at different times in different forms. This is the God who, because he took human form, took cosmic form. And the God who as source of beauty is found in beauty. The God who is revealed to us in that artistic creation we call Jesus Christ is also revealed to us in the artistic creation of each life and revealed to us in the artistic creations we print in books and hang on walls and build on streets.

Fringe people we are, yet so close to the centre of things. Only people who recognise distance can assess closeness to the centre. So we give thanks for that developed creative dimension in so many people that allows us to see the centrality of the fringe.

Two great Irish writers of this century, James Joyce and Samuel Beckett, had their own concept of the fringe existence. For all their distance from overt christianity, I like to think that they had something of the latent Church about them of which Paul Tillich spoke. Joyce himself focused on a fringe city of Europe, this city; on fringe people within it, an artist and a Jew, in a teeming, Catholic, one might say, philistine city. And out of that he has fashioned the novel that has changed the novel, the novel we call Ulysses; the extraordinary journey through the city and through the day that ends in the extraordinary soliloquy of Molly Bloom, with its final exultant 'Yes, I will, yes'. It is an affiration of life, of creativity, and finally if implicitly, I like to think, of the God of Life, the God of creation and creativity, the God of Jesus Christ.

The distance and the isolation are explored increasingly by Samuel Beckett in his 'isolates' from Murphy and Malone through Didi and Gogo, down to the nameless, even the bodiless people of some of his recent plays and novellas. The absurdity, the isolation, all call for the answer 'no' instead of Joyce's 'yes'. And yet as I read Beckett, he can never quite say 'no'.

Those two writers and artists of our own country and of our own century did, as I say, distance themselves from any formal church or christianity and yet, they are revealers of something of the Word that is made flesh and as they are revealers, they can be transformers. The revelation that was Jesus is a revelation for transformation, for new creation. So, it seems to me, is all great art. So, it seems to me, are all authentic human relationship and communication.

The move along the fringe, which Jesus took from Nazareth to Jerusalem and outside the gate to the Place of the Skull, is the critical revelation of who and what we are. As the critical revelation, it calls for the critical transformation of each of us as fringe pilgrims. Along the way we are helped by all the other revealers, saints and sinners, prosaic and poetic. We are helped in a special way, by artistic human creation which has celebrated and revealed so much of what is God and of what is good. As art reveals it challenges to further transformation and salvation.

Doubting Christians

Doubting Christians might seem a rather bold title in some respects. However, I frequently adapt a saying of the German writer Thomas Mann to theologians. Mann says about writers that they are people who find it very hard to write. I sometimes think theologians may be people who find it very hard to believe.

At least I consider that each of us has within himself or herself a certain questioning alter-ego; a certain sceptical self that is often asking us the hard questions, the hard questions about the meaning of life. Can we accept the meaning handed down or handed over? Can all this stuff about God and Jesus Christ and Church really makes any sense?

These questions cannot be simply evaded. They are part of us, part of us even in quiet times, in church itself or in boisterous times at home or in the pub. The questions may suffer us into thinking again about whether we really believe. I consider this questioning to be essential to the honesty of our belief and to its growth. The suppression of such questions in ourselves can undermine genuine christian faith. That is why the temptation to unbelief, the inability to accept such and such about God or Jesus or Church in ourselves, may be a grace for us. Shocking as it may sound it is also shocking us out of a certain comfortable, easy grasp of God whereby we make God to fit our wishes and do not face the challenge of the God of Abraham and the God of Jesus Christ. This God is above all a summons to truth. He is not something or somebody we can settle once for all saying, that's it, God exists, God's like this, I accept God. The unbelieving self reminds us that God cannot be settled in such a way. The unbelieving self is the self that helps to shatter many of our false gods as we translate God into some simple source of comfort for ourselves or some project of our own wishes and desires. The God who disturbed Israel and Abraham and Isaac, the God who took human form in Jesus Christ, is a very disturbing God, a shatterer of idols.

The questions keep coming. They are questions about our own

lives and deaths. They are questions, I think, that come to many of us when we lose a close friend or a member of the family. Can one relate to this member now? Has it any significance that she lived or died? Does faith keep the connection? Or is it simply a form of self-delusion?

There are even more distressing and challenging problems about us than an individual's death. The greatest challenge I experienced to my faith, in my work as a theologian, was a study I undertook some years ago of the attempted elimination of the Jews under the Nazi reign in Germany. The problem of evil as a whole is disturbing for us. Can there be a good and loving and all-powerful God and have even one child suffer? When we project it onto the scale of the Holocaust, the question becomes overwhelmingly disturbing.

One of my introductions to this was a book of memoirs by a Jewish survivor of the Holocaust called Elie Wiesel. In his book called Night he recounts when he first came to the camps:

> Never shall I forget that night, the first night in the camp, that has turned my life into one long night seven times cursed and seven times sealed. Never shall I forget that smoke. Never shall I forget the faces of the children whose bodies I saw turned into wreaths of smoke beneath the silent blue sky. Never shall I forget those flames which consumed my faith forever. Never shall I forget that nocturnal silence which deprived me for all eternity of the desire to live. Never shall I forget those movements which murdered my God and my soul and turned my dreams to dust. Never shall I forget these things, even if I am condemned to live as long as God himself. Never.

Facing the problem of God in the aftermath of Auschwitz, confronted by what became such a powerful parable of human evil, has been very difficult for many traditional believers, both Jewish and Christian. Can we still make sense of the God? Why was God silent? Where was God in Auschwitz?

Wiesel himself tells a very moving story that gives at least a part answer to the question. This is a very famous passage but it does bear repeating in confronting us with both the darkness or the absence of God and the possibility of presence:

One day when we came back from work we saw three gallows rearing up in the assembly place, three black crows. Roll-call. SS all round us. Machine guns raised. The traditional ceremony. Three victims in chains and one of them the little servant, the little Dutch boy, the sad-eyed angel. The SS seemed more preoccupied, more disturbed than usual. To hang a young boy in front of thousands of spectators was no light matter. The head of the camp read the verdict. All eyes were on the child. He was lividly pale, almost calm, biting his lips. The gallows threw its shadow over him. This time the lager kapo refused to act as executioner. Three SS replaced him. The three victims mounted together on to the gallows. The three necks were placed at the same moment within the nooses. 'Long live liberty!', shouted the adults, but the child was silent.

'Where is God? Where is he?' someone behind me asked. At a sign from the head of the camp the three chairs tipped over. Total silence throughout the camp. On the horizon the sunwas setting.

'Bear your heads!' yelled the head of the camp. His voice was raucous. We were weeping. 'Cover your heads!'

Then the march past began. The two adults were no longer alive. Their tongues hung swollen, blue-tinged, but the third rope was still moving. Being so light the child was still alive. For more than half-an-hour he stayed there, struggling between life and death, dying in slow agony under our eyes and we had to look him full in the face. He was still alive when I passed in front of him. His tongue was still red, his eyes not yet glazed.

Behind me I heard the same man asking, 'Where is God now?' And I heard a voice within me answer him, 'Where is he? Here he is. He is hanging there on this gallows.'

That night the soup tasted of corpses.

Finding God in the darkness, which some people at Auschwitz did, is part of our consolation; part of our way of realising that perhaps our images of God as somebody who simply interfered and ran the world his way, or else remained totally distant and indifferent. And it's part of the questioning that leads to the darkness, that may open us to some more of the reality of God; the God on the gallows.

Finding God in the darkness is what many of the great mystics and saints have been telling us of, over the centuries. But even they did not experience a darkness like Auschwitz. The God who comes through there is the God who suffered with the victims. The God of Calvary is continuing his compassionate role. He is suffering with.

That kind of question opens us to a somewhat different vision of God. The evil that men do is done to God. God takes on that evil in inexhaustible patience and power. The questioning moves us from a vision of a detatched demigod, to a much more significant power at the heart of our lives, at the heart of our suffering, and at the heart of our joy.

If we question we can grow. If the questions are honestly pursued, honestly faced, we can move from the childish God of our early faith, to a more significant power mediated to us, above all, in Jesus. But that is a very serious challenge to all of us. It is the challenge of God, the God who is the summons to further truth. This God who takes us beyond the tinsel and the wrappings, from some of our childish views of that old bearded figure in the sky, is a God who continues to call us beyond where we are. The summons to truth is the presence of God. It is an astonishing human phenomenon that we are summoned, continually summoned to truth; that we can tell the difference between truth and untruth; that while we may settle at times for untruth, we do not finally settle comfortably. It is the questioning self that rejects the comfort of falsehood and the untruth of teddy-bear gods that we hug to ourselves for our comfort, or wish to possess like toys for our use.

The Doubting Christian is a true christian, if the doubts come from the need and desire to find a fuller truth. We are not talking of an individualist phenomenon. We don't find truth or fuller truth simply on our own. The search for truth, like all our enterprises, is social as well as personal. It is communal, something we do in interaction with people. The heart of the central doctrine of christianity, the incarnation, is that God comes to us through one another. It is through one another, and with one another, dependent on one another, we carry on the search for the fuller truth. That summons to God may be the questioning neighbour as well as the questioning self. That finding of God may be the steadfast neighbour as well as the faithful self. It is in and through one another God calls us forward, and at the same time empowers us. We do not invent truth, we discover it. And the discovery of any truth is always some stage on the way to discovery of the fullness of truth, the final truth we call God. The empowerment and the summons in the search itself reflects the energy and capacity of God.

In the world in which we live it sounds ironic to suggest that the development of a certain scepticism is important to christians. The discovery or admission at least of our own questioning power is a discovery of a power for truth that is beyond all human control and possession. We settle in our politics, in our families, unfortunately often in our religion, for less than the truth. And yet, the God who called Abraham, the God who called Jesus, is always calling us to some of that fuller truth. There is too much truth for any of us or indeed for all of us together. But the authenticity of our lives, the genuineness, the sincerity, depend on listening to that call and carrying on in response with all the resources available to us. Above all we seek truth in community. The community of faith we call Church must be a community of truth and trust in which doubters too can come to the fuller truth.

Of course the Church has its own admixture of doubt and mistake. All of us as Church are sinful, ambiguous; in certain respects untruthful to our God and to ourselves. And yet it is the community that carries on the spirit of truth, that broke through so significantly with Jesus and has now to be part of our continuing story. We go through periods of darkness, both as persons and as communities. We go through these doubtful, difficult times. They can be prelude to breakthrough rather than breakdown. They can be our way to a new vision of life and a new vision of God. It's the breakthrough that is the critical grace. But breakdown or disruption of us in different ways in the course of our lives is necessary for the growth and transformation of breakthrough. The doubts that are grace, are the doubts that prepare us to leave the limited domestic gods of our previous life and open up to the richer fuller God who awaits us at the next stage.

It's that grace for breakthrough I think about as the grace of questioning. It's that kind of grace that affects all of us in different ways, at different times. But it's also that kind of grace that might cause us to panic with ourselves, or to be impatient or dismissive of the others. The community of truth, which we call Church, is meant to be a community of support, a community of resourcefulness and resources, a community of tolerance and acceptance. It is meant to mediate that God who is at once summoning us to fuller truth, and supporting and caring for us where we are.

In the *Irish Times* Francis Stuart published the following poem: it was called *The Love, The Loss, The Dream*.

I've never struck a bargain in my life,
Trafficking in the hardest currencies
I've mostly come away with tinsel trash,
But once or twice I've gained realities:
The bread, the wine, the love, the loss, the dream,
Though only at the staggering market price,
And finally I prayed, though not as bid:
'Lord, make me clean!'
But: 'Come and share with me my leper lair,
That's if you dare.'
And so he did.

The God who shares our leper lair, is the God who at once summons us to truth and loves us into truth. The summons is not a burden simply to be borne, although it has its difficulties. It is finally a loving grace to be enjoyed. For those of us who believe and half-believe, and would believe and yet doubt and wonder, in all these phases of our mind and heart, God's own finger, the finger of truth, is reaching to us. Truth to be given as grace, truth to set us free, is there. We need, at least at times, to relax into the God who shares our leprosy, the God who loves us in our very refusal: the God who is active in our very doubt. We need to relax with that God – to let him or her love us into the fuller truth that shall genuinely set us free.

Powerless Christians

I have adverted already in these meditations to the strange strategy
of God: the strange strategy of coming in the time of a great empire, ignoring the emperor, and even ignoring the centre of empire, and seeking out instead the tiny province of Israel and the
lost village of Nazareth. This strategy of God is not something
capricious or intended merely to divert us, or puzzle us. God seeking to break through to us, in presence and power to love and transform us, comes through the least ones. His way is not to convert
the emperor or to serve the powers of this world, but to identify
with the excluded and the impoverished, and the oppressed. He
does this not in order to leave them oppressed or as some kind of
masochist, taking on the sufferings of the human race. Coming
through the least, God can more easily be seen to be loving uncon-
ditionally. He comes for the sake of the people and not for the
sake of the power or the return. The divine strategy which fastens
on the powerless ones, as God's messengers, as God's witnesses to
the world, is about transforming the world, but, in the divine wisdom, it is through the people who could not easily think of themselves as God's people, still less as Godlike.

The final form of this breakthrough by God was the man from
Nazareth. And Jesus' message had, in Israel's terms, a traditional
ring, when he announced the 'coming of God's Kingdom or reign'.
It's a tricky word, 'Kingdom'. We think of it, and so did many of
Jesus' contemporaries, in terms of a territory, and a power, and a
political regime. But it was clear from all that Jesus said and did,
that he wanted to avoid that kind of understanding or rather misunderstanding. Yet even at the very end of his time, as he bade farewell to his disciples, he was questioned by those closest to him,
'Will you at this time restore the Kingdom of Israel?'(Acts 1:6).

The Kingdom or reign of God was not to be like the old kingdom of King David in Israel. It was not to be an alternative Roman
Empire in Jesus' in time. So Jesus kept clear of the Zealots, the
revolutionaries. It was to be an expression of God's presence and

God's power that would reveal God above all as transforming love; as taking up those bruised and broken, excluded and oppressed, and transforming them personally and in their relationships and structures.

Two strains of thought emerge in relation to this. One is the message and the ministry of Jesus as he sought out the non-respectable, the sick and the excluded. In his companionship with them, in eating and drinking with them, he showed a very different pattern from that which we normally follow when we are pleased to be invited to the table of the great; or seek to have them at our tables; when we are in that upwardly mobile club that tries to avoid the people further down. Jesus went to the bottom of the ladder and began his Kingdom there. To let it be seen that, as Mary in the Magnificat announced, 'the mighty are put down from their thrones and the lowly are exalted'.

That was one strand in the strategy and the message of Jesus. There was a direct criticism of the 'powers that be' also, whether they were religious powers or political powers. Jesus himself in so far as he was sharp, was sharp about the religious leaders of his own time, sharply critical of their seeking the first place in the synagogues, wearing their phylacteries broad, letting people see how good and holy and representative of God's power they were. The story of the Pharisee and the Publican is one powerful illustration of Jesus' recognition of God's strategy. He who sat at the back of the temple and said 'Lord, be merciful to me a sinner' went down to his house justified, transformed, emancipated. Criticism of the powers that be had, of course, to be transmitted and applied to his own disciples, who, as we read in Mark's gospel, just after his prediction of his own death, his death of rejection and execution, were still unheeding and unhearing enough to ask 'Who shall sit at your right hand and your left when you come into your Kingdom?' Jesus' criticism of that kind of ambition, and that kind of power, was direct and clear - that we will not lord it over them in this Kingdom as they did in the human political kingdoms of his time. The Son of Man came to serve and not to be served. His taking up the basin and water and towel in John's account of his farewell party, the Last Supper as we call it, his taking it up to wash his disciple's feet, is a symbol of the new different power of Jesus. People recognised this new power in Jesus. He spoke with authority and not as the other teachers of his time.

It is therefore an upside-down Kingdom that Jesus was

announcing in so far as the last should be first, the least of these should be raised up. The power exercised should be a power of service, of enabling and serving the others and not a power of dictation and manipulation; not an authoritarian power, political authoritarianism or ecclesiastical. Jesus, as the expression of God's presence, spent his time serving people, encouraging and enabling them to be more themselves, in comforting the bereaved and healing the sick, in driving out the demons and feeding the hungry. Jesus was about letting the deprived, the suffering, become more fully and truly themselves. He was not about leaving them in their suffering. He was not about endorsing their oppression. He was about emancipating and enabling. The power that is God's presence among us therefore is a power that, in and through Jesus, enables us in all our limitations.

There is something else revealed very clearly in the gospels: that the powerful themselves are trapped. Herod, moved by the dance of his daughter who asked for the head of John the Baptist, whom he respected, was caught in the trap. Pilot was entrapped: 'If you release this man you are not Caesar's friend.' The rich young man asked 'What last thing shall I do. I have kept all the commandments?' 'If you would follow me, give all that you have to the poor and come after me.' And he went away sad, trapped by his 'great possessions'.

That entrapment of wealth and power was very obvious to Jesus. Following out the divine strategy, he invited the wealthy and the powerful into the circle of the apparently powerless. The circle of the nobodies of this world that the loving power of God begins and where God is revealed as love opens up to include the rest of us. That's the circle that Jesus came to establish. Picking up the tradition of Israel, but breaking through it, he extended that circle from the deprived and oppressed of his own province to all the deprived and oppressed, and so to all of us. That's the upside-down dimension. But it isn't about leaving the deprived and oppressed as they are. It is about forming the divine circle in which we all share fully and equally by joining with the deprived and oppressed. That unity in Christ that Paul talked about so often, and talked about so clearly overcomes various kinds of oppression. For example, in his letter to the Galatians, he speaks of what has happened in Christ, that there are no longer Jew and Gentile – one obvious division and oppression; no longer slave and free – which was deeply built into the ancient world; no longer

male and female – a very obvious form of oppression in the world
of Paul and in our world today (Gal 3:28).

These barriers, the oppression and discrimination involved
in them, have been overcome in principle in that presence of God
we call his 'Kingdom', which took human form for us in Jesus
Christ. And it is that Kingdom or circle of God to which we are invited – that circle of the equal and free, where we no longer have
oppressor and oppressed, privileged and deprived. Here all of us
share equally in the basic goods of the earth. Here all of us share
equally in a 'setting free' way with one another. Here we are no
longer enslaved by our possessions or our ambitions or our apparent powers. We are fully with and for one another. It's a dream, of
course, yet a dream that, for example, sought christian expression
this week in Capetown. It's a dream that needs strong christian expression in this city. But it's not a dream in the sense of being un-
realisable; or even of being unreal.

The great tension of Jesus' preaching of the Kingdom was between the future realisation of the dream and the present realisation; the Kingdom that is already among you, as he said a number of
times, and the Kingdom for which we pray that it may come. It is a
basic tension in ourselves as persons and in our communities. But
the tension must not, as it were, be resolved by ignoring one or
other pole, and thinking that the dream is all about the future, the
future beyond death. It was, for Jesus, healing the sick, feeding the
hungry and preaching the 'good news' to the poor now. This was his
response, for example, to John's disciples who came back to ask
on behalf of John if he were the Messiah or 'must we wait for another?' It was along the same line he opened his own ministry in his
native village of Nazareth, reading from the Prophet Isaiah about
the good news for the poor and the healing and the helping to see
and the transformation of the world which he announced 'is this day
fulfilled in your hearing'.(Lk 4).

Jesus brought the Kingdom about in himself, his activities,
his community. His continuing community is called to further the
Kingdom. Not as if we can establish the final Utopia on earth.
But because here and now we are summoned to establish, in so far
as we can, the circle of God's children, in freedom and equality and
justice – headings picked up by many secular politicians later but
emerging very clearly in Jesus' own teaching.

In all this we are not to think of ourselves as simply
burdened. We are not to think of ourselves as primarily guilty.

There is a way of presenting the christian call to build the Kingdom 'now' in anticipation of the future, which can be simply
burdensome and guilt-inducing. That was not the dominant way of
Jesus. It should not be the dominant way of the Kingdom witnesses
and preachers today, because we are not on our own and we are not
the initiators.

If we open our eyes we find in so many places signs of the
Kingdom; summoning us to go farther, but also helping, encouraging, even enabling us. The love we experience, the justice we see
done, the truth we hear, the courage we see shown by many of these
deprived and oppressed; all of that is mediating Kingdom signals
and Kingdom powers. If we were to let God's presence loose among
us in our relationships with one another, personal and social or
structural, so much would flourish, so much would emerge. It's because we often have not the eyes to see God's enabling presence that
we withdraw under the burden and the guilt. Because we are not sensitive to, aware of the human others, even the most deprived, above
all, the most deprived others, as mediating this presence of God to
us we call Kingdom, we are afraid, afraid of further burdens, when
the message is for our liberation.

The message is for letting us be free with and for one another.
It is that kind of 'fringe faith' that is our releasing of God's reign
or Kingdom among us. Such faith is awareness of the mystery of
each human being, of the astonishing human capacity for love and
trust despite the astonishing destructive activities. It's openness
to what is going on about us in AIDS victims, in unemployed people, in people who are simply struggling with the day-to-day un-
dramatic difficulties. It's the recurrence of love among them and
by them. Like the fresh emergence of spring, such love reminds us
of the gift of the Kingdom, of the empowerment of it, of how it
enables us to begin to flourish again. We poke out little spring-
like buds, and begin in our faith to be liberated, to join that divine
circle. We enter into that remark-able company that Jesus
established as possible and real, and has on offer to us for 'no more
than the green leaf of our faith' - a phrase I adapted from this
poem called 'The Kingdom' by R.S. Thomas:

> It's a long way off but inside it
> There are quite different things going on:
> Festivals at which the poor man
> Is king, and the consumptive is

Healed; mirrors in which the blind look
At themselves and love looks at them
Back; the industry is for mending
The bent bones and the minds fractured
By life. It's a long way off, but to get
There takes no time and admission
Is free, if you will purge yourself
Of desire, and present yourself with
Your need only and the simple offering
Of our faith, green as a leaf.

That's the Kingdom that is on offer. That's the gift that can
be ours. That's the liberation to which we are invited, not on our
own but above all through those on the fringes of our lives, of our
society, of our world.

Forgotten Christians

One of the hazards of doing a series and taking rather striking titles to catch attention, like 'Creative Christians','Doubting Christians', 'Powerless Christians' and now, 'Forgotten Christians' is that one may be trying to exploit too much the striking-ness of the phrase rather than following through the truth that is on offer to us in Jesus Christ. Yet the forgotten christians, who find themselves in so many ways estranged in a world that has be-come so difficult to cope with, are multiple. They are the people who are widowed, bereaved in various ways, have lost family and friends. It is in many ways the age of the refugee, and the refugee that we think of in Africa or Asia or Latin America, is also symbolised and realised among ourselves as we take refuge from a changing world and find ourselves perhaps without friends and support. The sub-title suggested for this was 'Strangers in a Changed World'.

The great model of the forgotten, of the estranged, and a model to which I shall return, is the prisoner – the prisoner whom Christ came to set free in that programme announcement of his in the synagogue in Nazareth (Luke 4). Stephen Spender has a splendid poem on the prisoners which is relevant.

> Far, far the least of all, in want,
> Are these,
> The Prisoners
> Turned massive with their vaults and dark with dark.
> They raise no hands, which rest upon their knees,
> But lean their solid eyes against the night,
> Dimly they feel
> Only the furniture they use in cells.
> Their time is almost Death. The silted flow
> Of years on years
> Is marked by dawns
> As faint as cracks on mud-flats of despair....

It is too late for anger,
Nothing prevails
But pity for the grief they cannot feel.

These physical prisoners, the prisoners in our gaols, the
prisoners in gaols around the world, are a sign to us of our own
estrangement and imprisonment, our own difficulty in making
contact, our own loneliness. How many kinds of prisoners, or how
many kinds of forgotten are there in our Church, in our city and in
our country?

And what is happening to them? The mud-flats of despair may
not affect all of these prisoners or forgotten, but there is often a
great lack of hope. There is a loss of expectation, a resignation at
the nothingness, they think, is about them and is also, they fear,
ahead of them.

But the forgotten have a counterpart in the forgetters, the
people who forget. What happens to the forgotten in their
estrangement and loneliness has its own counterpart in those who
forget. We think of our memory as an important part of ourselves.
Our ability to remember our names, to remember our past, to
remember where we are and how we came here, is essential to our
identity. Lapses in memory, its disappearance in some kind of diseased amnesia, would undermine completely our personal lives. If
we did not know who we are, if our individual identity went with the
forgettingness, we would not count, and could not be counted. Job
speaks of 'no name in the street'. This was adopted by James
Baldwin for a cry of near despair about the forgotten blacks of
Harlem. Our forgetting could have the same effect on us.

That forgetting which enters into us if we let go of our past,
enters into us in another way, if we let go of our present, above all
if we let go of the presence of people. If we do not remember who
they are, we rapidly lose sight of who we are. We belong with them.
We are members of a family, of a community. We belong to an
Irish society. We belong to a Western society. We belong to a
diminishing one world. If we forget these things; if above all, we
forget these people who constitute our family and our society and
our world, we are lapsing out of identity. Because it's our relationships in the family and the community, and the wider world,
that structure us, make us the people we are today. We don't exist
in separation from the past or else we lose our identity. We lose
hold of who we are. So it is with the present and its people. It is as

if we are locked into, or hooked up to the range of people who are
present with us in the world, our co-human beings. And we only
become ourselves in relationship, in conscious relationship and
interaction with them. If we would simply forget them, if we were
to cut ourselves off in some perverse fit of snobbery, or in some
diseased paranoia that they were all out to get us, or simply in lazy
evasion of the demands they might make upon us, we would in fact
destroy who we were.

The destruction of the forgotten has its counterpart in the
destructiveness that affects the forgetters. We sometimes for our
comfort quote the remark that the English never remember and the
Irish never forget. It would seem these March days to be fulfilled
more than ever. But it is in fact part of a larger problem, part of a
larger reality that the top people, those who 'take' the Times,
don't have to remember. Indeed it's in their interest to forget. But
the bottom people are never allowed to forget. So the forgetting
that affects so many of us in the First World in relation to the
Third, in the employed in relation to the unemployed, in the not so
old in relation to the elderly, in the healthy in regard to the ill, in
the free in regard to the prisoners, the forgetfulness that affects
all of us is partly in our interest. Partly it enables us to evade the
challenge of the others. But if it does so, it also deprives us of the
potential enrichment of meeting that challenge. It deprives us of
the rich presence of the others. It secludes us in our own self-
constructed prison. We are afraid to leave that prison. We build
the walls higher. We are afraid of the freedom wherewith Jesus has
set us free (Gal 5:1).

And of course Jesus is, in this as in so many other issues, at
the heart of the matter: 'Come to set prisoners free' as he
announced in adapting to himself the saying of the prophet Isaiah.
He himself manifested that freedom by being with the sick and the
excluded in various ways – the forgotten people of his own Israel.
But remembering was part of the tradition he inherited. 'Remember Israel' is a continuously ringing cry through the Old
Testament. 'Remember your God ... remember your covenant ... remember your orphans, your poor, your strangers.' That call to remember, echoed by so many different prophetic voices, emanates
ultimately from Yahweh the God of Israel. For Yahweh remembers
and he expects us to reflect that remembering. But Jesus took it up
in his own unique way as we read, 'on the night before he died he
came together with his disciples and he took bread and wine and he

gave them to eat and to drink, for this, he said, is my body which is given and broken for you, this is my blood which is shed for you; do this in memory of me'. In memory of Jesus. In memory of the body that was given and broken, of the blood that was shed. In memory of the end of a career; one might say the glorious failure of a career – from prophet, anticipated Messiah for many, to executed criminal deserted by his disciples.

If top people are tempted to forget, and above all to forget bottom people, then the Eucharist ought to be the cure, the reminder, the source of transformation. The criteria of success, the way we might wish to be remembered, as successful, as the successful who write the history, all that has been radically undermined by the peculiar failure, success/failure of Jesus Christ. It is the victim, not the victimisers we are to remember.

Remembering for christians is of this supreme victim. The remembering that we do in the Eucharist is not just of the individual victim, Jesus of Nazareth. If we are to be true to him, the remembering is to be of all victims, of all the forgotten. He himself underlined this, in the story we read in St Matthew's Gospel of the final judgement (Mt 25). The prisoners and the sick, the hungry and the thirsty, the least ones, bottom people, victims of all our structures – these are the presence of us, of Jesus. 'As long as you did it to one of these least ones you did it to me.' We are not really believing in the real presence of Jesus in the Eucharist if we are not alert to his real presence in the least ones, if we do not remember them in our lives, if we do not keep them in mind. If we do not let that keeping in mind be a source of response to them, we are not keeping the Jesus of the Eucharist in mind. We are not really accepting this real presence.

Of course none of us is able for all this remembering. We have our limitations. These limitations we use as our protective barriers. They are our excuse, our reason for refusing the freedom that would take us to be with the lonely and the lost. It must be by these others, who are the contemporary victims reflecting Jesus' exclusion and victimisation, that we are empowered and set free. Not that we can meet all these victims face to face, any more than we meet the victim, Jesus, face to face. But the lack of face-to-face contact should not be lack of contact. It should not be lack of connection which leads to freedom and salvation.

In human and in christian terms our unwillingness to make the connections, to accept the presence of the others in our

immediate circle, but finally in our worldwide circle; our convenient forgetfulness, will lead us to the left-hand side of the Son of
Man in that story in St Matthew's Gospel, 'depart from me, for I
was hungry and you did not give me to eat'.

It is a challenge that can be overwhelming. It can lead us to
visualise 'our own mud-flats of despair'. But there is no divine
challenge without power; no summons from God without the grace
of enablement. Jesus is not about binding insupportable burdens.
He is about enabling, about liberating us. We become more fully
and truly ourselves, as these others are accepted, acknowledged,
responded to, many in face-to-face relationships, many, many
more in the structural relationships of our own society and the
great world beyond. In and through these structural relationships,
political, social, economic and cultural, we pick up the signals
of the presence of Jesus among isolated widows or starving
Ethiopians or prisoners under torture and so receive his transforming power.

These signals we hear are the sacraments of contemporary
victims. The real presence of Jesus Christ is also in the isolated
and deprived who are all about us. In struggling to respond, we are
summoning up the resources God has given us, the Eucharistic and
faith resources, the human resources. We are summoning up in
order that we may not forget who the victims are and so finally
forget who we are. As we do that, out of the grace that is given us in
Eucharist, and in so many other ways; as we are enabled to respond,
we raise a flag of hope above 'the mud-flats of despair'. 'Our pity
for the grief they cannot feel' examines our lack of feeling as it
attempts to raise that sign of hope in a world so badly in need of it.

If, in our struggle for this better world, we offer significant
signs of hope to these people; if they begin to see that the Jesus
who came to set prisoners free, is actually at work among us and
among them, then the hope that is in them will in turn enliven our
faith. If our meagre efforts for that kind of world, for the emergence of the upside-down kingdom, ignites their hope, their very
presence to us ignites our faith. Attending to these people is a
source of faith to us. It's an enlargement of our awareness and understanding of Jesus Christ and of the God of Jesus Christ. The bit
we do to offer christian hope in the world opens us up to those
fringe people, those forgotten and excluded, from whom and
through whom our faith will be renewed. It was from the excluded
and forgotten victim, Jesus Christ, that our faith was born in the

first instance. Overcoming our forgetfulness is a growth in faith. It's an opening up to the real presence of God and of Jesus in the world in which we live.

In this series we struggled with the idea of 'faith at the fringe'. We may at least take away one simple message – attention to the people at the fringes of our lives, above all those deprived and forgotten by so many, is the way of renewal for our faith. It's the way through to Jesus Christ and his God.

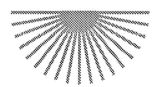

Conclusion

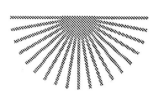

The Final Question: Does Death Matter?

'So death, the most terrifying of ills, is nothing to us, since so long as we exist, death is not with us; but when death comes, then we do not exist. It does not then concern either the living or the dead, since for the former it is not, and the latter are no more' (Epicurus).

The cruder, popular notion of Epicureanism, an injustice to the rather sensible and sensitive ancient philosopher, should not obscure the persisting intellectual attraction of this ancient Greek's view of death. In the more austere vision of one of the most influential philosophers of this century, Ludwig Wittgenstein, 'Death is not an event of life. Death is not lived through.' This is connected with his later remark, 'whereof one cannot speak, thereof one must be silent'.

Silent before the mystery, or dismissive of an insoluble puzzle, these philosophers reflect a human and philosophical reluctance to engage intellectually with that most incontrovertible of truths, that we shall all die. Although death has been described as the muse of philosophy, it is only recently that it has begun to play a serious role in philosophising. Schopenaeur, the eighteenth century Dutch Jewish philosopher, may have been the first modern philosopher to confront it. In this century, despite Wittgenstein's monitum, philosophers with existentialist preoccupations have made it a central issue. Camus suggested that suicide was the only serious philosophical issue. Sartre saw death in all its absurdity as rendering the human being a 'useless passion'. Heidegger, giant among existentialists, viewed it as entering into human existence as a challenge to authenticity and a shaper of identity. For these twentieth-century Western philosophers, death does matter, although in radically diverse ways.

Twentieth-century Western literature inherited a much stronger tradition dealing with death. From Homer and Horace to Donne and Dostoevsky, poets, dramatists and novelists have wrestled with 'proud death'. While William Empson may, in his poem 'Ignorance of Death', 'feel very blank about this topic', Hemingway in his bull-ring, Joyce among his Dubliners and Lorca asking 'If I die/Leave the balcony open' are more typical of a fascination, romantic or sardonic, accepting or protesting, with this century's fifty-seven varieties of death and dying. The century which gave us the horrors of the trenches in World War I, the technical perfection of carpet-bombing in World War II, with Auschwitz and Hiroshima topping the bill, to be followed by some one hundred and fifty destructive wars since 1945, intermingled with famines on a scale to make our Irish experience seem so limited, and now compounded by ecological destruction and the spectre of Aids, such a century could hardly produce a serious literature which took Empson's way of 'feeling blank on this topic' rather than Dylan Thomas's 'Rage against the dying of the light'. Yet the scale may be too grand. Thomas, like most writers, concentrates on individual death. The Holocaust mocks most literary efforts to comprehend it. The film *Hiroshima, Mon Amour* and its creative parallels proceed by indirection, a well-tried literary device in face of individual death, of which Thomas Hardy's 'The Walk' offers an excellent example:

> You did not walk with me
> Of late to the hill-top tree
> By the gated ways,
> As in earlier days;
> You were so weak and lame
> So you never came.
> And I went alone, and I did not mind,
> Nor think of you as left behind.
>
> I walked up there today
> Just in the former way;
> Surveyed around
> The familiar ground
> By myself again:
> What diference then?
> Only that underlying sense
> Of the look of a room on returning thence.

A collection of short stories about the Aids crisis, *The Darker Proof*, (Adam M. Jones and Edmund White, Faber, 1987) is more explicit and direct than Hardy and yet maintains a discretion that allows for mystery and a death which matters.

Such delicate discretion and indirection have been crowded off stage, screen and page by what Geoffrey Gorer has called 'The pornography of Death' as this century's major response to death. Integral to the cheapening thrill is the final meaninglessness of death and so of life. The disjunction of death and the appropriate human emotion of mourning is what Gorer describes as pornography, analogous to the disjunction of sex and love in sexual pornography. Such sexual rituals as our civilisation offers, in prettifying corpses and other death-disguises, promote this disjunction in the same way as Rambo violence on the screen and a cost-effective corpse-count on the battlefield or in the gas-chamber do. Evasion of other people's death is frequently matched in our culture by attempts to evade our own. Evasive attitudes, clearly as old as Epicurus, have reached for new technological expressions, of which the freezer-programme is clearly the most bizarre. Such stratagems of evasion only serve to underline how, even for those most endowed with the good things of life, perhaps particuarly for those, death still matters, but is concealed.

The self at risk

To dare speak about death in philosophical and theological fashion is to risk judgement on one's own evasiveness, to put one's own authentic self-hood, as Heidegger might say, at risk. Self-indulgent agonising about personal attitudes to death are no less inauthentic than evasion. What the self believes and fears and even hopes has to reach for the distance of Donne in his 'Death be not proud' without adopting the apparent detachment of Philip Larkin:

Hours giving evidence
Or birth, advance
On death, equally slowly
and saying so to some
Means nothing; others it leaves
Nothing to be said.

'Born astride the grave' in Beckett's phrase, this self cannot avoid the taste and threat of nothingness. From nothingness – to nothingness. From nothingness certainly – of that I have no doubt.

CONCLUSION   149

Continually threatened with nothingness, with the huge silence
that is death, that was the clear lesson of this morning's car journey
as it is of so many other modern moves and moods. That 'tumult in
the clouds' which so attracted Yeats' Irish airman, is re-enacted on
terra firma without necessarily involving his joyous conclusion:

> The years to come seemed waste of breath,
> A waste of breath, the years behind
> In balance with this life, this death.
> *An Irish Airman Foresees his Death*

Despite the dangers of romanticising, evident here and open
to us all in our recurring adolescent moods, the tenuous hold each
has on existence can break through at any time. In more specula-
tive vein, the gap between being and non-being which life and death
embody for us, can spark off a kind of intellectual vertigo which
is, to say the least, unbalancing. Falling off the edge of the cliff
may be the conventional metaphor for the lapse into the nothingness from which we came. As with so many great clichés, it has an
original and devastating power of communication. The self, the
alert self-aware self, the self which cherishes life and each living
moment, is both frightened and excited as it peers over the edge of
the cliff, as it peers into the abyss. For all the fearful prospects
on every side of the tight-rope walker, the living self has its energies at once concentrated and more creatively released, its joy and
living enhanced by the very threats which surround it. That death
looms in this way, to strike often in arbitrary and unpredictable
ways, can in certain reflective moods be seen to provide a depth
and authenticity to living which a more pedestrian view and a more
vegetative existence could miss. The nothingness behind and
around and before the self can, as Heidegger discerned, give human
existence a tautness and a concentration which brings the particular self together in face of its particular journey to death. Nothingness, non-being, destination death can compel attention, focus
energies, call the self to be somebody before it disintegrates into
inevitable no-body.

A serious limitation of this line of thinking, valuable as it
may be in exposing certain nerve-ends of the self's existence, is its
utterly individualist attitude to death. Deaths like 'sorrows, come
not single spies but in battalions'. The twentieth-century is the
witness supreme to that, whether the battalions were in the

trenches, the concentration camps, the bombed-out cities or the famine-stricken regions. So much attention to individual dying and death in the era of Somme, Auschwitz, Nagasaki and Ethiopia seems to this self inexcusably individualistic and a luxury feasible only in the comfortable developed world. What can an individual death matter among the statistical horrors reaching us from every decade of this century and from every quarter of the globe? The risk of nuclear holocaust, pollution of the environment with its concomitant health risks, particularly widespread death patterns through cancer and heart disease and the still more sinister threat of Aids, are forcing the wealthy and privileged societies to consider anew, or for the first time, their solidarity in dying. The corporate threat and reality of death is coming home to many people in ways that the self cannot easily accommodate, certainly not the post-Enlightenment autonomous self of the West or his sophisticated successor, the existentialist self. The post-Revolutionary self of the Eastern bloc countries has been exposed to the opposite risk, total submersion of the self in the collective with the triumph of the proletariat, more precisely of the Party, and more precisely still of the party leaders and apparatchiks. The death of the individual, disgraced leader or purged peasant and peasant masses, means as little in that context as six million Jews or hundreds of thousands of Vietnamese gooks mattered in the communist-free West.

This self is unable to escape the impact of these mass deaths. The personal self comes into existence and matures in a series of overlapping and ever-widening communities, if the spatial images are not getting too confused. What happens through famine in Ethiopia, through war in the Gulf, through torture and execution in Chile, through Aids in the US or through murderous republicanism and unionism in Northern Ireland, affects this self. In varying degrees such destruction puts this self at risk, not least the risk of indifference and apathy with their own death-dealing inauthenticity and disintegration. For the self to live in face of these corporate death phenomena, it must protest and confront them. For the self to die, physically or morally in its authentic connections with the wider community, that is another blow to the living human community within which every human self must have its being. The communal, corporate dimensions of life and death continue to challenge our most profound philosophical analyses.

The romantics and the existentialists may have been weak on

the communal character of death. They were strong on commitment. This was of course primarily commitment to life, indeed, for existentialists like Camus, a defiance of death, as life was taken on in all its 'heroic absurdity'. Commitment to life carried a heavily individualist overtone but it was nonetheless authentic in its cherishing the life of other individuals, as Camus' hero Dr Rieux in The Plague powerfully illustrates. A further appreciation of the commitment involved in the fuller existence of the personal self in community opens up the reality of personal trust and entrustment. Without trust in others, without self-entrustment to others, personal existence is impossible or becomes the hell of isolation and suspicion which Sartre misunderstood so profoundly in *Huis Clos*. Community depends on trust. Person depends on community and helps create community through trust. Human living, personal and communal, operates properly out of and into trust.

And human dying? Samuel Beckett's isolates, dying as they eke out their existences, convey so much of contemporary mistrust in their living-dying. Company, Beckett's beautifully judged ironic and not quite desolate novella, rehearses all the doubts and hesitations of the abandoned in search of, and utterly distrustful of, the companionship of a human voice, his own or another's, addressing him or another. The trust that is essential to human living is essential to human dying with all the rich implications for family and friends, for doctor and patient. If one cannot always 'go gently into that good night', one should be helped to go trustingly. The most effective help for this is a trusting life in a trusted and trusting community.

The self may still rebel. Dissolution can be so fearsome, although there are moments in many people's lives when they simply wish to cease to be, after life's fitful fever simply to sleep, well or ill. It would be foolish to dismiss the attractions of 'easeful death' in particular circumstances. How one responds to them depends in large measure on how one has responded to life, on one's larger view of life and its meaning. That larger view will be considered in the final section of this paper. This also applies to those who rebel against dying, as so many do. The larger view, for example, the christian view, does not inevitably overcome the attractions of too easily accepting or persistently rejecting the fact of one's death. A tangential comment derived from Karl Mannheim and translated into personal terms by Karl Rahner may help. Mannheim asks what kind of society would we have if there were no death? The absence of death would clearly matter enormously but with what consequences for our continuing society? Karl Rahner, in a more personal comment over a beer, could not see the value of indefinite human living. Would it prevent people from bringing their lives to a point, and so achieving some life-stance and commitment, in Heideggerian terms? Would it, in Mannheim's conception, create intolerable obstacles to the maturity and creativity of succeeding generations and perhaps exclude the trust that also implies each generation and individual shall have a fair share of the goods of the earth and of the direction of the community? Is the option for the freezer an attempt to provide raw material for Mannheim's concept?

Christ has died

The human response to death has traditionally been a religious one. It still is for most people around the world and even for many incorporting or infected by (depending on your viewpoint) Western secular ideas. The Western religious response has its roots in either Judaism or its derivative Christianity. Although earlier Jewish thought experienced very interesting developments in the interpretation of death, and especially in relation to the destiny of the dead, I shall confine myself to some reflections on the response of christians as they seek to understand and integrate, into their own living and dying, the life and death of Jesus Christ. For christians, this life and death provide the way to understanding their own. Four or five related aspects of the destiny of Jesus merit discussion here.

(i) A human life and death

The Jesus of the Gospels, for all the difficulties of interpret- ation, was not a pseudo-human being. He lived a truly human life and died a truly human death. This is hard to keep in mind in view of his own recorded claims and of his followers' developing belief. Yet it is essential to the Gospel account and indeed to the value and validity of the claims and beliefs.

That human living was a full and exciting one, with its mission of proclaiming and inaugurating God's kingdom or reign in the world. This kingdom was to take community shape, the shape of love of God and of neigbour, with particular attention to the poor and excluded, the deprived and handicapped. Jesus' teaching

CONCLUSION 153

and ministry gave abundant evidence of all this, sufficient evidence at any rate to disturb the Jewish religious leaders and finally their Roman political masters. The price of Jesus' dedication in truth and love to the oppressed, to the lame and the blind, to the poor (Luke 4) was his own life. If they were to have life, he must surrender his.

Jesus was aware of his impending doom. While he went freely to Jerusalem to confront it, he entered into the final process reluctantly and fearfully. 'If it be possible, let this chalice pass from me' in the garden. More desperately on the cross, 'My God, my God, why hast thou forsaken me?' Yet the trusting, accepting, loving side prevailed: in the garden, 'Not my will but thine be done' to the Father, and 'Let these go their way' of his disciples to those who would arrest him. On the cross he completed his trusting surrrender to the Father, 'Into thy hands I commend my spirit' while he sought reconciliation with his fellow-victim, 'This day thou shalt be with me in Paradise' and with his persecutors, 'Father forgive them, for they know not what they do'. In laying down his life for the others, Jesus, and in christian faith, through Jesus, God, took on all the fearful destructiveness of dying and death. The nothingness before which so many quail has been confronted and encountered by the man Jesus who was the Son of God. Part at least of the christian response to death of self and of others, even of the multitude of others in famine and in war, is that God in Jesus has been here before and is here now. Whatever is happening in human dying is also happening to and with the God of Gethsemane and Calvary.

(ii) Christ has risen

Because God was with Jesus in dying and death, death could not prevail. 'On the third day he rose again.' In the more expressive language of Paul, Jesus was raised by God from the dead. Acceptance of death in love and trust issued in the overcoming of death in new life, in resurrection. Here christianity departed from some of the Greek influences already apparent in some Jewish thinking and widely influential beyond. It was not Jesus' soul which enjoyed new life after its escape from his body, as it were. It was the true, human person of Jesus, which had truly died and which was now truly raised. It was the embodied Jesus then, not his purely spiritual soul which was experienced by the disciples as alive. Whatever one makes of this risen spiritual body, (*soma pneumati-*

kon in Paul's phrase), what is at issue is not a Platonic or Neo-
platonic release of a soul from a body, but the transformation of a
total human person. Our philosophical and theological
limitations in elaborating the further implications of this should
not blind us to the clear teaching of the New Testament.

(iii) Body of Christ and Communion of Saints

The full human being who was Jesus Christ was never an
isolated individualist. Dying for his friends (and enemies), he was
raised as the 'first fruits of resurrection' (1Cor 15). The Body of
Christ, a key phrase of Paul, had many members who were reborn by
sharing his death in baptism and so his resurrection. In their own
historical dying they completed their baptismal sharing and
entered into fullness of communion with Christ. Resurrection was
already seen as a corporate and community reality, expressed by
the later church in terms of the communion of saints. As the
christian should not die alone but in and with Jesus Christ, in and
with the body of Christ on earth, the loving community of disciples and friends, she is not raised alone but enters into the community of the blessed with Christ. Living with and for one another
moves through dying with and for one another into the new life with
and for one another.

(iv) A new heaven and a new earth

The transformation of life, with its community significance
which Jesus' resurrection anticipates for all, is not, in New Testament terms, a merely human phenomenon. The whole of creation
is involved (Rom 8). Human continuity with the cosmos heralds,
in christian thinking, cosmic transformation of a kind as yet unin-
telligible to us but already demanding respect for the cosmos in
ecological caring. The complete human being, personal, communal and cosmic, is called to the destiny of resurrection, to
eschatological fulfilment in eternal life.

(v) Eternal life

A simple juxtaposition of the synoptic Gospel accounts of
Jesus' life, death and resurrection, of Paul's wrestling with the
power and presence of the risen Christ, and of John's focus on the
gift of eternal life which is already present in christians, suggests
a new perspective on christian fulfilment and the meaning of
christian dying. What Jesus achieved for all in overcoming death

and dying, new life, fullness of life, eternal life, is already in action in human beings. It is not something available only beyond death. By baptism or its equivalent, loving human beings share the death and new life of Christ (Paul). The kingdom is already within them (Synoptics).

This is eternal life: to know God and Jesus Christ whom he has sent (John 17:3). Such life is one of commitment, trust and love. Dying is to be the final maturing of that commitment, trust and love in the context of a committed, trusting and loving community with a care for the cosmos. Premature death and dying is precisely that – premature and to be protested and resisted by the committed, trusting and loving community. The eternal life, of which the christian community is already conscious, compels them, as it compelled Jesus, to go out to those prematurely and unjustly exposed to destruction by famine or war, by medical neglect or arbitrary accident. The call of and to eternal life is a call heard in this life for the protection and promotion of historical human life. In our commitment to the human life of all, particulary the most deprived, christians manifest the eternal life that is in them. In their final dying they seek to communicate this sense of eternal life, this love and trust, which helps to overcome the fears of those about them, fears of death and bereavement. The dying are in turn supported by the love and trust, the eternal life at work in their families and in those who care for them. The dying's final act of trust in God is born of and borne by their trusting supporters. Eternal life can only be fully attained in such dying. The Mannheim nightmare of a society with no death would finally frustrate this thrust to eternal life, which as christians understand, is now at the loving, trusting heart of authentic human community. As a crucial and cruciform stage on the way of life, to final fullness of life, death does matter to christians.

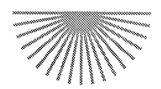